Investment Banking Workbook

Investment Banking Workbook

JOSHUA ROSENBAUM

JOSHUA PEARL

WILEY

ISBN 978-1-118-45611-8 (Paperback); ISBN 978-1-118-65621-1 (cloth);
ISBN 978-1-118-28125-3 (cloth + models);
ISBN 978-1-118-47220-0 (paper); ISBN 978-1-118-41985-4 (ebk);
ISBN 978-1-118-42161-1 (ebk); ISBN 978-1-118-69505-0 (ebk)

Printed in the United States of America

10 9 8 7 6 5 4 3 2 1

Contents

About the Authors

JOSHUA ROSENBAUM is a Managing Director at UBS Investment Bank in the Global Industrial Group. He originates, structures, and advises on M&A, corporate finance, and capital markets transactions. Previously, he worked at the International Finance Corporation, the direct investment division of the World Bank. He received his AB from Harvard and his MBA with Baker Scholar honors from Harvard Business School.

JOSHUA PEARL is an investment analyst at Brahman Capital Corp. Previously, he structured and executed leveraged loan and high yield bond financings, as well as leveraged buyouts and restructurings as a Director at UBS Investment Bank in Leveraged Finance. Prior to UBS, he worked at Moelis & Company and Deutsche Bank. He received his BS in Business from Indiana University's Kelley School of Business.

CONTACT THE AUTHORS

Please feel free to contact JOSHUA ROSENBAUM and JOSHUA PEARL with any questions, comments, or suggestions for future editions at **josh@investmentbankingbook.com**.

Acknowledgments

We would like to highlight the contributions made by **Joseph Gasparro** toward the successful production of this workbook. His contributions were multi-dimensional and his unwavering enthusiasm, insights, and support were nothing short of exemplary. In general, Joe's work ethic, creativity, "can-do" attitude, and commitment to perfection are a true inspiration. We look forward to great things from him in the future.

We would also like to thank **Ezra Faham** for all his efforts and contributions in the completion of this workbook.

Acknowledgments

Introduction

This workbook is designed for use both as a companion to our book, *Investment Banking: Valuation, Leveraged Buyouts, and Mergers & Acquisitions, Second Edition*, as well as on a standalone basis. *Investment Banking* focuses on the primary valuation methodologies currently used on Wall Street—namely, comparable companies analysis, precedent transactions analysis, discounted cash flow (DCF) analysis, and leveraged buyout (LBO) analysis, as well as detailed mergers & acquisitions (M&A) analysis from both a sell-side and buy-side perspective. Our workbook seeks to help solidify knowledge of these core financial topics as true mastery must be tested, honed, and retested over time. We envision the workbook being used as a self-help tool for students, job seekers, and existing finance professionals, as well as in formal classroom and training settings.

The workbook provides a mix of multi-step problem set exercises, as well as multiple choice and essay questions. We also provide a comprehensive answer key that aims to truly teach and explain as opposed to simply identify the correct answer. Therefore, the answers themselves are an effective learning tool. The level of difficulty for these exercises and questions ranges from basic to advanced. The format of the workbook is designed to optimize mastering the critical financial tools discussed in *Investment Banking* and therefore corresponds to its chapters, as shown below:

- Chapter 1: Comparable Companies Analysis
- Chapter 2: Precedent Transactions Analysis
- Chapter 3: Discounted Cash Flow Analysis
- Chapter 4: Leveraged Buyouts
- Chapter 5: LBO Analysis
- Chapter 6: Sell-Side M&A
- Chapter 7: Buy-Side M&A

TARGET AUDIENCE

We are confident that this workbook will enable users to take their learning to the next level in terms of understanding and applying the critical financial tools necessary to be an effective finance professional. Consequently, our target audience for the workbook overlaps with *Investment Banking*—namely current and aspiring investment bankers, students, career changers, private equity and hedge fund professionals, sell-side research analysts, and finance professionals at corporations (including members of business development, finance, and treasury departments). We also believe our workbook is highly beneficial to those attorneys, consultants, and accountants focused on M&A, corporate finance, capital raising, and other transaction advisory services.

At the same time, our workbook is designed to serve as the ultimate teaching tool for finance professors, instructors, and trainers. The multiple choice questions are complemented by rigorous multi-step exercises designed to ensure mastery of key modeling conventions and financial calculations. It is the perfect complement to classroom or online instruction, as well as core course reading materials. In fact, *Investment Banking* and this workbook are designed in an integrated manner so as to provide a foundation around which a professor, instructor, or trainer can build an entire course.

CONTENT AND APPLICATIONS

The multi-step exercises are instrumental for learning the calculations and modeling skills behind the core valuation, LBO, and M&A tools. Once mastered, these exercises provide a solid foundation for financial modeling (including crafting financial projections), and performing comparable companies, precedent transactions, DCF and LBO Analysis, as well as comprehensive merger consequences analysis (including the creation of pro forma financial statements). They also provide a sound understanding of more complex calculations and nuances involving accretion/(dilution) analysis, exchange ratios, premiums paid, treasury stock method (TSM), capital asset pricing model (CAPM), weighted average cost of capital (WACC), goodwill, tangible and intangible write-ups, deferred tax liabilities, and numerous other critical topics.

The multiple choice questions are designed to be used on both an individual as well as collective basis. In other words, individual questions from each chapter can be mixed and matched to accommodate any testing, learning, or training format. At the same, taken collectively for a given financial topic, the questions and exercises provide an integrated and multidimensional approach that can be used to teach and learn the material, whether individually, in the classroom, or for a training program.

CHAPTER 1

Comparable Companies Analysis

1) Using the information provided for Gasparro Corp., complete the questions regarding fully diluted shares outstanding

General Information	
Company Name	Gasparro Corp.
Ticker	JDG
Stock Exchange	NYSE
Fiscal Year Ending	Dec-31
Moody's Corporate Rating	Baa3
S&P Corporate Rating	BBB-
Predicted Beta	1.25
Marginal Tax Rate	*38.0%*

(shares in millions)

Assumptions	
Current Share Price	$50.00
Basic Shares Outstanding	98.50

Options/Warrants		
Tranche	Number of Shares	Exercise Price
Tranche 1	1.250	$10.00
Tranche 2	1.000	30.00
Tranche 3	0.500	40.00
Tranche 4	0.250	60.00

a. Calculate Gasparro Corp.'s in-the-money options/warrants

_____

b. Calculate proceeds from in-the-money options/warrants

_____

c. Calculate net new shares from the options/warrants

_____

    d. Calculate fully diluted shares outstanding

2) Using the prior answers and information, as well as the balance sheet data below, calculate Gasparro's equity value and enterprise value

($ in millions, except per share data)

Assumptions	
Current Share Price	$50.00
52-week High Price	62.50
52-week Low Price	40.00
Dividend Per Share (MRQ)	0.25

Balance Sheet Data	2011A	9/30/2012
Cash and Cash Equivalents	$75.0	$100.0
Accounts Receivable	625.0	650.0
Inventories	730.0	750.0
Prepaids and Other Current Assets	225.0	250.0
Total Current Assets	**$1,655.0**	**$1,750.0**
Property, Plant and Equipment, net	1,970.0	2,000.0
Goodwill and Intangible Assets	775.0	800.0
Other Assets	425.0	450.0
Total Assets	**$4,825.0**	**$5,000.0**
Accounts Payable	275.0	300.0
Accrued Liabilities	450.0	475.0
Other Current Liabilities	125.0	150.0
Total Current Liabilities	**$850.0**	**$925.0**
Total Debt	1,875.0	1,850.0
Other Long-Term Liabilities	500.0	500.0
Total Liabilities	**$3,225.0**	**$3,275.0**
Noncontrolling Interest	-	-
Preferred Stock	-	-
Shareholders' Equity	1,600.0	1,725.0
Total Liabilities and Equity	**$4,825.0**	**$5,000.0**
Balance Check	*0.000*	*0.000*

  a. Calculate equity value

b. Calculate enterprise value

3) Using the information provided for Gasparro, complete the questions regarding non-recurring items

Non-recurring Items

$25.0 million pre-tax gain on the sale of a non-core business in Q4 2011
$30.0 million pre-tax inventory valuation charge in Q2 2012 related to product obsolescence
$15.0 million pre-tax restructuring charge in Q3 2012 related to severance costs

($ in millions, except per share data)

Reported Income Statement

	Fiscal Year Ending December 31,			Prior Stub 9/30/2011	Current Stub 9/30/2012	LTM 9/30/2012
	2009A	2010A	2011A			
Sales	$3,750.0	$4,150.0	$4,500.0	$3,375.0	$3,600.0	$4,725.0
COGS (incl. D&A)	2,450.0	2,700.0	2,925.0	2,200.0	2,350.0	3,075.0
Gross Profit	$1,300.0	$1,450.0	$1,575.0	$1,175.0	$1,250.0	$1,650.0
SG&A	750.0	830.0	900.0	675.0	720.0	945.0
Other Expense / (Income)	-	-	-	-	-	-
EBIT	$550.0	$620.0	$675.0	$500.0	$530.0	$705.0
Interest Expense	110.0	105.0	102.0	75.0	73.0	100.0
Pre-tax Income	$440.0	$515.0	$573.0	$425.0	$457.0	$605.0
Income Taxes	167.2	195.7	217.7	161.5	173.7	229.9
Noncontrolling Interest	-	-	-	-	-	-
Preferred Dividends	-	-	-	-	-	-
Net Income	$272.8	$319.3	$355.3	$263.5	$283.3	$375.1
Effective Tax Rate	*38.0%*	*38.0%*	*38.0%*	*38.0%*	*38.0%*	*38.0%*
Weighted Avg. Diluted Shares	100.0	100.0	100.0	100.0	100.0	100.0
Diluted EPS	$2.73	$3.19	$3.55	$2.64	$2.83	$3.75

Cash Flow Statement Data

	Fiscal Year Ending December 31,			Prior Stub 9/30/2011	Current Stub 9/30/2012	LTM 9/30/2012
	2009A	2010A	2011A			
Cash From Operations	400.0	450.0	500.0	360.0	380.0	520.0
Capital Expenditures	170.0	185.0	200.0	150.0	155.0	205.0
% sales	*4.5%*	*4.5%*	*4.4%*	*4.4%*	*4.3%*	*4.3%*
Free Cash Flow	$230.0	$265.0	$300.0	$210.0	$225.0	$315.0
% margin	*6.1%*	*6.4%*	*6.7%*	*6.2%*	*6.3%*	*6.7%*
FCF / Share	$2.30	$2.65	$3.00	$2.10	$2.25	$3.15
Depreciation & Amortization	155.0	165.0	175.0	125.0	125.0	175.0
% sales	*4.1%*	*4.0%*	*3.9%*	*3.7%*	*3.5%*	*3.7%*

a. Calculate adjusted LTM gross profit for Gasparro, assuming the $30.0 million inventory charge is added back to COGS

    b. Calculate adjusted LTM EBIT

    c. Calculate adjusted LTM EBITDA

    d. Calculate adjusted LTM net income

4) Using the prior answers and information, complete the questions regarding Gasparro's LTM return on investment ratios

    a. Calculate return on average invested capital

    b. Calculate return on average equity

    c. Calculate return on average assets

    d. Calculate implied annual dividend per share

5) Using the prior answers and information, complete the questions regarding Gasparro's LTM credit statistics

    a. Calculate debt-to-total capitalization

        _____

    b. Calculate total debt-to-EBITDA

        _____

    c. Calculate net debt-to-EBITDA

        _____

    d. Calculate EBITDA-to-interest expense

        _____

    e. Calculate (EBITDA – capex)-to-interest expense

        _____

    f. Calculate EBIT-to-interest expense

        _____

6) Using the prior answers and information, calculate Gasparro's trading multiples

($ in millions, except per share data)

Trading Multiples				
	LTM 9/30/2012	NFY 2012E	NFY+1 2013E	NFY+2 2014E
EV / Sales	A)	1.4x	1.3x	1.2x
Metric	$4,725.0	$5,000.0	$5,350.0	$5,625.0
EV / EBITDA	7.5x	B)	6.6x	6.3x
Metric	$900.0	$950.0	$1,025.0	$1,075.0
EV / EBIT	9.3x	8.8x	C)	7.8x
Metric	$725.0	$765.0	$825.0	$865.0
P/E	12.9x	11.2x	10.0x	D)
Metric	$3.88	$4.45	$5.00	$5.50
FCF Yield	6.3%	7.0%	7.5%	E)
Metric	$315.0	$350.0	$375.0	$415.0

a. Calculate Gasparro Corp.'s LTM enterprise value-to-sales

b. Calculate 2012E enterprise value-to-EBITDA

c. Calculate 2013E enterprise value-to-EBIT

d. Calculate 2014E P/E

e. Calculate 2014E FCF yield

7) Using the prior answers and information, calculate Gasparro's growth rates

Growth Rates	Sales	EBITDA	FCF	EPS
Historical				
1-year ('10-'11)	A)	5.1%	13.2%	6.4%
2-year CAGR ('09-'11)	9.5%	B)	14.2%	11.6%
Estimated				
1-year ('11-'12E)	11.1%	15.2%	C)	31.0%
2-year CAGR ('11-'13E)	9.0%	11.5%	11.8%	D)

a. Calculate Gasparro's historical one-year sales growth

_____

b. Calculate historical two-year EBITDA compounded annual growth rate

_____

c. Calculate estimated one-year FCF growth

_____

d. Calculate estimated two-year EPS CAGR

_____

8) Using the information provided for ValueCo's peers, complete the questions regarding LTM profitability margins

($ in millions, except per share data)

| | LTM Financial Statistics | | | | | LTM Profitability Margins | | | |
Company	Sales	Gross Profit	EBITDA	EBIT	Net Income	Gross Profit (%)	EBITDA (%)	EBIT (%)	Net Income (%)
BuyerCo	$6,559.6	$2,328.7	$1,443.1	$1,279.1	$704.8	A)	22%	20%	11%
Sherman Co.	5,894.6	1,945.2	1,047.0	752.2	419.3	33%	B)	13%	7%
Pearl Corp.	4,284.5	1,585.3	838.7	624.5	325.2	37%	20%	C)	8%
Gasparro Corp.									
Kumra Inc.	3,186.7	922.4	665.3	505.9	248.4	29%	21%	16%	D
Mean						**32%**	E)	**16%**	**8%**
Median						**36%**	**20%**	F)	**8%**

a. Calculate BuyerCo's gross profit margin

---

b. Calculate Sherman Co.'s EBITDA margin

---

c. Calculate Pearl Corp.'s EBIT margin

---

d. Calculate Kumra Inc.'s net income margin

---

e. Calculate the mean EBITDA margin

---

f. Calculate the median EBIT margin

---

9) Using the information below, calculate the LTM leverage and coverage ratios for ValueCo's peers

($ in millions)

LTM Financial Data

Company	Debt	Market Cap	Cash	Int. Exp.	Capex	EBITDA	EBIT
BuyerCo	$2,200.0	$2,480.0	$400.0	$142.4	$196.8	$1,443.1	$1,279.1
Sherman Co.	3,150.0	2,359.0	649.0	76.0	235.8	1,047.0	752.2
Pearl Corp.	1,500.0	2,559.6	815.6	100.0	128.5	838.7	624.5
Kumra Inc.	891.2	2,687.6	481.3	60.3	143.4	665.3	505.9

	LTM Leverage Ratios			LTM Coverage Ratios		
	Debt / Tot. Cap.	Debt / EBITDA	Net Debt / EBITDA	EBITDA / Int. Exp.	EBITDA - Cpx/ Int.	EBIT / Int. Exp.
Company	(%)	(x)	(x)	(x)	(x)	(x)
BuyerCo	A)	1.5x	1.2x	10.1x	8.8x	9.0x
Sherman Co.	57%	B)	2.4x	13.8x	10.7x	9.9x
Pearl Corp.	37%	1.8x	C)	8.4x	7.1x	6.2x
Gasparro Corp.						
Kumra Inc.	25%	1.3x	0.6x	D)	E)	F)
Mean	**44%**	**G)**	**1.4x**	**10.5x**	**8.4x**	**8.2x**
Median	**47%**	**1.8x**	**1.2x**	**H)**	**8.7x**	**8.4x**

a. Calculate BuyerCo's debt-to-total capitalization (using market value of equity)

b. Calculate Sherman Co.'s debt-to-EBITDA ratio

c. Calculate Pearl Corp.'s net debt-to-EBITDA ratio

d. Calculate Kumra Inc.'s EBITDA-to-interest expense ratio

e. Calculate Kumra Inc.'s (EBITDA – capex)-to-interest expense ratio

f. Calculate Kumra Inc.'s EBIT-to-interest expense ratio

g. Calculate the mean debt-to-EBITDA leverage ratio

h. Calculate the median EBITDA-to-interest expense ratio

10) Using the information below, calculate the LTM valuation multiples for ValueCo's peers

($ in millions, except per share data)

LTM Financial Data

Company	Sales	EBITDA	EBIT	EPS
BuyerCo	$6,559.6	$1,443.1	$1,279.1	$5.03
Sherman Co.	5,894.6	1,047.0	752.2	2.99
Pearl Corp.	4,284.5	838.7	624.5	4.31
Kumra Inc.	3,186.7	665.3	505.9	2.70

Company	Current Share Price	Equity Value	Enterprise Value	Enterprise Value / LTM Sales	Enterprise Value / LTM EBITDA	Enterprise Value / LTM EBIT	Price / LTM EPS
BuyerCo	$70.00	$9,800.0	$11,600.0	A)	8.0x	9.1x	13.9x
Sherman Co.	40.00	5,600.0	8,101.0	1.4x	B)	10.8x	13.4x
Pearl Corp.	68.50	5,171.8	5,856.1	1.4x	7.0x	C)	15.9x
Gasparro Corp.							
Kumra Inc.	52.50	4,851.6	5,344.6	1.7x	8.0x	10.6x	D)
Mean				1.5x	E)	9.8x	15.1x
Median				1.4x	7.7x	9.4x	F)

a. Calculate BuyerCo's enterprise value-to-sales multiple

b. Calculate Sherman Co.'s enterprise value-to-EBITDA multiple

   c. Calculate Pearl Corp.'s enterprise value-to-EBIT multiple

_____

   d. Calculate Kumra Inc.'s P/E multiple

_____

   e. Calculate the mean enterprise value-to-EBITDA multiple

_____

   f. Calculate the median P/E ratio

_____

11) Using the information below, calculate ValueCo's implied valuation ranges using the company's LTM EBITDA

($ in millions, except per share data)

EBITDA	Financial Metric	Multiple Range		Implied Enterprise Value		Less: Net Debt	Implied Equity Value		Fully Diluted Shares	Implied Share Price	
LTM	$700	7.0x	– 8.0x	A)	–A)	(1,500)	B)	–B)	80	C)	–C)

   a. Calculate ValueCo's implied enterprise value range

_____

   b. Calculate ValueCo's implied equity value range

_____

   c. Calculate ValueCo's implied share price range

_____

12) Using the information below, calculate ValueCo's implied valuation ranges using the company's LTM net income

($ in millions, except per share data)

Net Income	Financial Metric	Multiple Range		Implied Equity Value		Fully Diluted Shares	Implied Share Price	
LTM	$258	13.0x – 16.0x	A)	–A)		80	B)	–B)

   a. Calculate ValueCo's implied equity value range

        _____

   b. Calculate ValueCo's implied share price range

        _____

13) Which of the following is the correct order of steps to complete comparable companies analysis?

    I. Locate the Necessary Financial Information
    II. Select the Universe of Comparable Companies
    III. Spread Key Statistics, Ratios, and Trading Multiples
    IV. Determine Valuation
    V. Benchmark the Comparable Companies

    A. II, I, III, V, IV
    B. I, II, III, IV, V
    C. II, I, III, IV, V
    D. III, I, IV, V, IV

14) All of the following are business characteristics that can be used to select comparable companies EXCEPT

    A. Products and Services
    B. Distribution Channels
    C. Return on Investment
    D. Sector

15) All of the following are financial characteristics that can be used to select comparable companies EXCEPT

    A. Credit Profile
    B. Growth Profile
    C. Profitability
    D. Geography

16) Which of the following are key business characteristics to examine when screening for comparable companies?

    I. Sector
    II. Return on investment
    III. End markets
    IV. Distribution channels
    V. Return on assets

    A. I and III
    B. II and IV
    C. I, III, and IV
    D. I, II, III, IV, and V

17) Which of the following are key financial characteristics to examine when screening for comparable companies?

    I. Customers
    II. Profitability
    III. Growth profile
    IV. Credit profile
    V. End markets

    A. II and III
    B. II, III, and IV
    C. I, II, and IV
    D. II, III, and V

18) End markets refer to the

    A. Market into which a company sells its products and services
    B. Medium through which a company sells its products and services to the end user
    C. End users of a product or service
    D. Stores that distribute a company's product or service

19) Distribution channels refer to the

   A. Market into which a company sells its products and services
   B. Medium through which a company sells its products and services to the end user
   C. End users of a product or service
   D. Stores that distribute a company's product or service

20) Which of the following is NOT a financial statistic to measure the profitability of a company?

   A. Gross margin
   B. EBITDA margin
   C. EBIT margin
   D. Equity margin

21) Which of the following is NOT a source for locating financial information for comparable companies?

   A. 10-K
   B. 13-D
   C. Investor Presentations
   D. Equity Research

22) Which of the following is the correct calculation for fully diluted shares outstanding when used in trading comps?

   A. "Out-of-the money" options and warrants + "in-the-money" convertible securities
   B. Basic shares outstanding + "in-the-money" options and warrants + "in-the-money" convertible securities
   C. "In-the-money" options and warrants + "in-the-money" convertible securities
   D. Basic shares outstanding + "out-of-the money" options and warrants

23) Which methodology is used to determine additional shares from "in-the-money" options and warrants when determining fully diluted shares?

   A. Treasury Stock Method
   B. "If-Converted Method"
   C. Net Share Settlement Method
   D. "In-the-Money" Method

24) Calculate the company's equity and enterprise value, respectively, using the information below

($ in millions, except per share data; shares in millions)

Assumptions	
Current Share Price	$20.00
Fully Diluted Shares	50.0
Total Debt	250.0
Preferred Stock	35.0
Noncontrolling Interest	15.0
Cash and Cash Equivalents	50.0

A. $1,000.0 million; $1,250.0 million
B. $1,000.0 million; $1,350.0 million
C. $1,700.0 million; $1,915.0 million
D. $1,700.0 million; $1,350.0 million

25) Calculate fully diluted shares using the information below

($ in millions, except per share data; shares in millions)

Assumptions	
Current Share Price	$25.00
Basic Shares Outstanding	200.0
Exercisable Options	20.0
Weighted Average Exercise Price	$10.00

A. 150.4 million
B. 200.5 million
C. 212.0 million
D. 220.0 million

26) Calculate fully diluted shares using the information below

($ in millions, except per share data; shares in millions)

Assumptions	
Current Share Price	$40.00
Basic Shares Outstanding	300.0
Exercisable Options	10.0
Weighted Average Exercise Price	$26.00

A. 295.4 million
B. 300.0 million
C. 303.5 million
D. 310.0 million

27) If a company has an enterprise value of $1,000 million and equity value of $1,150 million, what is the company's net debt?

    A. $250 million
    B. ($250) million
    C. $150 million
    D. ($150) million

28) What is the most conservative (most dilutive scenario) way to treat options and warrants when calculating fully diluted shares outstanding?

    A. Use all outstanding "in-the-money" options and warrants
    B. Use all exercisable "in-the-money" options and warrants
    C. Ignore all "in-the-money" options and warrants
    D. Ignore all outstanding "in-the-money" options and warrants

29) Which type of "in-the-money" options may be excluded from the calculation of fully diluted shares outstanding in comparable companies analysis?

    A. Exercisable
    B. Net share settled
    C. Outstanding, but not exercisable
    D. If-Converted

30) Calculate fully diluted outstanding shares using the information below

($ in millions, except per share data; shares in millions)

Assumptions	
Company	
Current Share Price	$45.00
Basic Shares Outstanding	250.0
Convertible	
Amount Outstanding	$300.0
Conversion Price	$30.00

    A. 200.5 million
    B. 253.8 million
    C. 260.0 million
    D. 265.5 million

31) Calculate fully diluted shares using the information below

($ in millions, except per share data; shares in millions)	
Assumptions	
Current Share Price	$30.00
Basic Shares Outstanding	350.0
Exercisable Options	10.0
Weighted Average Exercise Price	$15.00
Convertible Amount Outstanding	$250.0
Convertible Conversion Price	$20.00

A. 325.0 million
B. 355.3 million
C. 363.5 million
D. 367.5 million

Use the information below to answer the next two questions

($ in millions, except per share data; shares in millions)	
Assumptions	
Current Share Price	$30.00
Conversion Price	$22.50
Convert Amount Outstanding	$225.0

32) Using the if-converted method, calculate net new shares

A. 2.5
B. 5.0
C. 10.0
D. 12.5

33) Using the net share settlement method, calculate net new shares

A. 2.5
B. 5.0
C. 10.0
D. 12.5

34) What is the formula for calculating enterprise value?

A. Equity value + total debt
B. Equity value + total debt + preferred stock + noncontrolling interest – cash
C. Equity value + total debt – preferred stock – noncontrolling interest – cash
D. Equity value + total debt + preferred stock + noncontrolling interest + cash

35) All else being constant, how does enterprise value change if a company raises equity and uses the entire amount to repay debt?

    A. Stays constant
    B. Increases
    C. Decreases
    D. Not enough information to answer the question

36) Show the necessary adjustments and pro forma amounts if a company issues $200.0 million of equity and uses the proceeds to repay debt (excluding fees and expenses).

($ in millions)

Issuance of Equity to Repay Debt				
	Actual 2012	Adjustments +	-	Pro forma 2012
Equity Value	$1,200.0			
Plus: Total Debt	750.0			
Plus: Preferred Stock	100.0			
Plus: Minority Interest	50.0			
Less: Cash and Cash Equivalents	(100.0)			
Enterprise Value	**$2,000.0**			

37) Which company below has a higher gross profit margin?

($ in millions)

Company A		Company B	
Revenue	$400.0	Revenue	$1,000.0
COGS	250.0	COGS	550.0

    A. Company A
    B. Company B
    C. Same margin for both companies
    D. Not enough information to answer the question

38) Using the information below, calculate the CAGRs for the 2010 – 2012 and 2012 – 2014 periods

				Fiscal Year Ending December 31,				
	2010A	2011A	2012A	CAGR ('10 - '12)	2013E	2014E	CAGR ('12 - '14)
Diluted EPS	$1.35	$1.60	$1.80		$2.00	$2.20	
% growth		18.5%	12.5%		11.1%	10.0%	

    A. 15.5% and 10.6%
    B. (13.4%) and (9.3%)
    C. 13.4% and 9.3%
    D. 13.0% and 9.0%

39) Which of the following is NOT a metric used to measure a company's growth?

    A. Long-term EPS growth rate
    B. Historical EPS CAGRs
    C. EBITDA margins
    D. y/y sales growth rates

40) Calculate the company's return on invested capital (ROIC)?

($ in millions)

Assumptions	
EBIT	$150.0
Net Debt	275.0
Shareholders' Equity	475.0
Goodwill	200.0
Capex	50.0

    A. 19.1%
    B. 20.0%
    C. 24.7%
    D. 30.0%

41) Calculate the company's return on equity (ROE)?

($ in millions)

Assumptions	
EBIT	$150.0
Net Income	85.0
Net Debt	300.0
Shareholders' Equity	315.0

    A. 10.0%
    B. 10.4%
    C. 27.0%
    D. 29.1%

42) Calculate the company's return on assets (ROA)?

($ in millions)

Assumptions	
EBIT	$200.0
Net Income	150.0
Net Debt	250.0
Shareholders' Equity	450.0
Total Assets	625.0

    A. 19.4%
    B. 22.4%
    C. 24.0%
    D. 25.2%

43) Calculate the company's debt-to-total capitalization

($ in millions)	
Assumptions	
Debt	$200.0
Preferred Stock	195.0
Noncontrolling Interest	50.0
Equity	675.0
Cash	100.0

A. 17.9%
B. 19.7%
C. 20.5%
D. 23.0%

44) When calculating an interest coverage ratio, which of the following is NOT used in the numerator?

A. Net income
B. EBIT
C. EBITDA
D. (EBITDA – capex)

45) Ratings of Aaa, Aa1, and Aa2 belong to which ratings agency?

A. S&P
B. Moody's
C. Fitch
D. SEC

46) Which of the following ratings is investment grade?

A. Ba1
B. BB+
C. BB-
D. BBB-

47) What is the Moody's equivalent of B+?

A. B1
B. B2
C. Ba1
D. Baa1

48) Calculate LTM 9/30/2012 sales given the information below

($ in millions)

Sales Data	
YTD 9/30/2012 Sales	$1,600.0
YTD 9/30/2011 Sales	1,450.0
YTD 9/30/2010 Sales	1,375.0
2011 Sales	2,250.0
2010 Sales	2,000.0

A. $1,900.7 million
B. $2,000.5 million
C. $2,100.0 million
D. $2,400.0 million

49) Calculate LTM 12/31/2012 sales given the information below

($ in millions)

Sales Data	
YTD 6/30/2012 Sales	$2,500.0
YTD 6/30/2011 Sales	2,350.0
YTD 6/30/2010 Sales	2,150.0
2012 Sales	4,250.0
2011 Sales	4,000.0

A. $2,500.0 million
B. $4,250.0 million
C. $4,000.0 million
D. $4,400.0 million

50) Calendarize the 4/30/2012 sales figure into a CY 2012 statistic so it can be used alongside companies reporting on a calendar year basis

($ in millions)

Sales Data	
FY 4/30/2013E Sales	$1,650.0
FY 4/30/2012A Sales	1,500.0
FY 4/30/2011A Sales	1,350.0

A. $1,050.5 million
B. $1,550.0 million
C. $1,600.0 million
D. $1,655.5 million

51) Calculate adjusted net income, EBITDA, and EPS, respectively, assuming $50 million of D&A, and adjusting for the $10.0 million restructuring charges as well as an inventory write-down of $5 million

($ in millions, except per share data)

Income Statement	
	Reported 2012
Sales	**$1,000.0**
Cost of Goods Sold	625.0
Gross Profit	**$375.0**
Selling, General & Administrative	230.0
Restructuring Charges	10.0
Operating Income (EBIT)	**$135.0**
Interest Expense	35.0
Pre-tax Income	**$100.0**
Income Taxes @ 40%	40.0
Net Income	**$60.0**
Weighted Average Diluted Shares	30.0
Diluted Earnings Per Share	$2.00

A. $60.0 million, $185.0 million, $2.00
B. $69.0 million, $200.0 million, $2.30
C. $60.0 million, $200.0 million, $2.00
D. $69.0 million, $185.0 million, $2.30

52) The P/E ratio is equivalent to

A. Equity value/net income
B. Enterprise value/net income
C. Enterprise value/EBITDA
D. Share price/free cash flow

53) Which of the following is not an appropriate valuation multiple?

A. Enterprise value/EBITDA
B. Enterprise value/EBIT
C. Enterprise value/net income
D. Enterprise value/sales

54) Which of the following is not an appropriate valuation multiple?

A. Equity value/EBITDA
B. Enterprise value/EBITDAR
C. Equity value/book value
D. Enterprise value/resources

55) Which statement contains the data on noncontrolling interest?

    A. Income statement
    B. Balance sheet
    C. Cash flow statement
    D. Management discussion & analysis

56) The two most generic and widely used valuation multiples are

    I. Enterprise value/EBITDA
    II. EBITDA/interest expense
    III. Total debt/EBITDA
    IV. P/E

    A. I and III
    B. I and IV
    C. II and III
    D. II and IV

57) What is the premise behind comparable companies analysis?

_____

_____

_____

_____

58) Two companies are very similar in terms of business characteristics, but they are currently trading at substantially different multiples. What discrepancies in financial characteristics could explain this situation?

_____

_____

_____

_____

59) All else being equal, which company would be expected to trade at a higher multiple—a heavily leveraged company or one with moderate to low leverage? Why?

_____

_____

_____

_____

60) Why are comparable companies sometimes tiered into different groups?

_____

_____

_____

_____

61) Match the SEC forms with their formal name

10-K	Proxy statement
10-Q	Annual report
8-K	Current report
DEF14A	Quarterly report

62) Match the valuation multiples with the appropriate sector

Enterprise value/reserves	Retail
Enterprise value/EBITDAR	Financial Institutions
Enterprise value/subscriber	Metals & mining
Price/Book	Media

63) What are some of the benefits of using comparable companies analysis?

_____

_____

_____

_____

64) What are some of the considerations when using comparable companies analysis?

_____

_____

_____

_____

1) Calculation of fully diluted shares outstanding

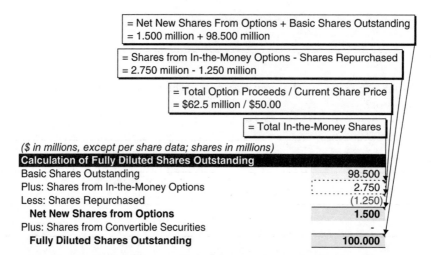

= Net New Shares From Options + Basic Shares Outstanding
= 1.500 million + 98.500 million

= Shares from In-the-Money Options - Shares Repurchased
= 2.750 million - 1.250 million

= Total Option Proceeds / Current Share Price
= $62.5 million / $50.00

= Total In-the-Money Shares

($ in millions, except per share data; shares in millions)

Calculation of Fully Diluted Shares Outstanding	
Basic Shares Outstanding	98.500
Plus: Shares from In-the-Money Options	2.750
Less: Shares Repurchased	(1.250)
Net New Shares from Options	**1.500**
Plus: Shares from Convertible Securities	-
Fully Diluted Shares Outstanding	**100.000**

Options/Warrants

Tranche	Number of Shares	Exercise Price	In-the-Money Shares	Proceeds
Tranche 1	1.250	$10.00	1.250	$12.5
Tranche 2	1.000	30.00	1.000	30.0
Tranche 3	0.500	40.00	0.500	20.0
Tranche 4	0.250	60.00	-	-
Tranche 5	-	-	-	-
Total	**3.000**	-	**2.750**	**$62.5**

= Tranche 1 In-the-Money Shares
+ Tranche 2 In-the-Money Shares
+ Tranche 3 In-the-Money Shares
= 1.250 million + 1.000 million + 0.500 million

= IF (Weighted Average Strike Price < Current
Share Price, display Number of Shares,
otherwise display 0)
= IF ($10.00 < $50.00, 1.250, 0)

= Tranche 1 In-the-Money Proceeds
+ Tranche 2 In-the-Money Proceeds
+ Tranche 3 In-the-Money Proceeds
= $12.5 million + $30.0 million + $20.0 million

= IF (In-the-Money Shares > 0, then
In-the-Money Shares x Weighted Average
Strike Price, otherwise display 0)
= IF (1.250 > 0, 1.250 x $10.00, 0)

a. 2.75 million. The total number of in-the-money options/warrants is calculated by adding the in-the-money shares from the tranches which have an exercise price lower than the current share price of $50.00. (1.250 million shares + 1.000 million shares + 0.500 million shares)

b. $62.5 million. The total proceeds from in-the-money options/warrants is calculated by adding the proceeds from the tranches which have an exercise price lower than the current share price of $50.00. ($12.5 million + $30.0 million + $20.0 million)

c. 1.50 million. Under the TSM, the $62.5 million of potential proceeds received by Gasparro is used to repurchase shares that are currently trading at $50.00. Therefore, the number of shares repurchased is 1.25 million ($62.5 million / $50.00) of the options. To calculate net new shares, the shares repurchased are subtracted from the total number of in-the-money options/warrants. (2.75 million shares – 1.25 million shares)

d. 100.0 million. Fully diluted shares are calculated as net new shares plus basic shares outstanding. (98.5 million shares + 1.50 million shares)

2) Calculation of equity value and enterprise value

($ in millions, except per share data; shares in millions)

Selected Market Data		
Current Price	12/20/2012	$50.00
% of 52-week High		*80.0%*
52-week High Price	7/20/2012	62.50
52-week Low Price	4/5/2012	40.00
Dividend Per Share (MRQ)		0.25
Fully Diluted Shares Outstanding		100.000
Equity Value		**$5,000.0**
Plus: Total Debt		1,850.0
Plus: Preferred Stock		-
Plus: Noncontrolling Interest		-
Less: Cash and Cash Equivalents		(100.0)
Enterprise Value		**$6,750.0**

= Equity Value + Total Debt - Cash
= $5,000.0 million + $1,850.0 million - $100.0 million

= Current Share Price x Fully Diluted Shares Outstanding
= $50.00 x 100.0 million

a. $5,000.0 million. Equity value is calculated by multiplying fully diluted shares by the current share price. (100.0 million shares × $50.00)

b. $6,750.0 million. Enterprise value is calculated as equity value plus total debt less cash and cash equivalents. ($5,000.0 million + $1,850.0 million – $100.0 million)

3) Adjusting for one-time and non-recurring items

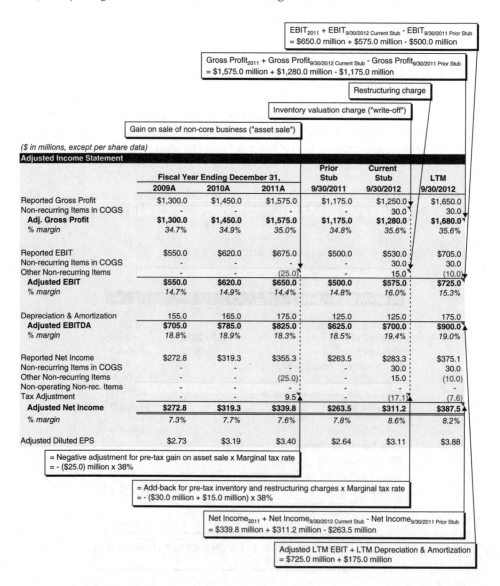

EBIT$_{2011}$ + EBIT$_{9/30/2012\ Current\ Stub}$ - EBIT$_{9/30/2011\ Prior\ Stub}$
= $650.0 million + $575.0 million - $500.0 million

Gross Profit$_{2011}$ + Gross Profit$_{9/30/2012\ Current\ Stub}$ - Gross Profit$_{9/30/2011\ Prior\ Stub}$
= $1,575.0 million + $1,280.0 million - $1,175.0 million

Restructuring charge

Inventory valuation charge ("write-off")

Gain on sale of non-core business ("asset sale")

($ in millions, except per share data)

Adjusted Income Statement

	Fiscal Year Ending December 31,			Prior Stub	Current Stub	LTM
	2009A	2010A	2011A	9/30/2011	9/30/2012	9/30/2012
Reported Gross Profit	$1,300.0	$1,450.0	$1,575.0	$1,175.0	$1,250.0	$1,650.0
Non-recurring Items in COGS	-	-	-	-	30.0	30.0
Adj. Gross Profit	**$1,300.0**	**$1,450.0**	**$1,575.0**	**$1,175.0**	**$1,280.0**	**$1,680.0**
% margin	*34.7%*	*34.9%*	*35.0%*	*34.8%*	*35.6%*	*35.6%*
Reported EBIT	$550.0	$620.0	$675.0	$500.0	$530.0	$705.0
Non-recurring Items in COGS	-	-	-	-	30.0	30.0
Other Non-recurring Items	-	-	(25.0)	-	15.0	(10.0)
Adjusted EBIT	**$550.0**	**$620.0**	**$650.0**	**$500.0**	**$575.0**	**$725.0**
% margin	*14.7%*	*14.9%*	*14.4%*	*14.8%*	*16.0%*	*15.3%*
Depreciation & Amortization	155.0	165.0	175.0	125.0	125.0	175.0
Adjusted EBITDA	**$705.0**	**$785.0**	**$825.0**	**$625.0**	**$700.0**	**$900.0**
% margin	*18.8%*	*18.9%*	*18.3%*	*18.5%*	*19.4%*	*19.0%*
Reported Net Income	$272.8	$319.3	$355.3	$263.5	$283.3	$375.1
Non-recurring Items in COGS	-	-	-	-	30.0	30.0
Other Non-recurring Items	-	-	(25.0)	-	15.0	(10.0)
Non-operating Non-rec. Items	-	-	-	-	-	-
Tax Adjustment	-	-	9.5	-	(17.1)	(7.6)
Adjusted Net Income	**$272.8**	**$319.3**	**$339.8**	**$263.5**	**$311.2**	**$387.5**
% margin	*7.3%*	*7.7%*	*7.6%*	*7.8%*	*8.6%*	*8.2%*
Adjusted Diluted EPS	$2.73	$3.19	$3.40	$2.64	$3.11	$3.88

= Negative adjustment for pre-tax gain on asset sale x Marginal tax rate
= - ($25.0) million x 38%

= Add-back for pre-tax inventory and restructuring charges x Marginal tax rate
= - ($30.0 million + $15.0 million) x 38%

Net Income$_{2011}$ + Net Income$_{9/30/2012\ Current\ Stub}$ - Net Income$_{9/30/2011\ Prior\ Stub}$
= $339.8 million + $311.2 million - $263.5 million

Adjusted LTM EBIT + LTM Depreciation & Amortization
= $725.0 million + $175.0 million

a. $1,680.0 million. To calculate adjusted LTM gross profit first add back the $30.0 million non-recurring product obsolescence charge to COGS for the current stub 9/30/2012 period. LTM gross profit is then calculated by taking the full prior fiscal year's gross profit, adding the YTD gross profit for the current year period ("current stub"), and then subtracting the

YTD gross profit from the prior year ("prior stub"). ($1,575.0 million + $1,280.0 million − $1,175.0 million)

b. $725.0 million. To calculate adjusted LTM EBIT first add back the $15.0 million restructuring charge and back out the $25.0 million gain on asset sale for the current stub 9/30/2012 period and fiscal year 2011 period, respectively. Next, the LTM statistic is calculated in the same manner as shown in 3(a). ($650.0 million + $575.0 million − $500.0 million)

c. $900.0 million. To calculate adjusted LTM EBITDA, add LTM depreciation and amortization to LTM EBIT. ($725.0 million + $175.0 million)

d. $387.5 million. To calculate adjusted LTM net income, first add back the full non-recurring charges to net income. Then, to make the tax adjustment, multiply the full add back amount by Gasparro's marginal tax rate. Next, the LTM statistic is calculated in the same manner as shown in 3(a). ($339.8 million + $311.2 million − $263.5 million)

4) Return on investment ratios

LTM Return on Investment Ratios	
Return on Invested Capital	21.1%
Return on Equity	23.3%
Return on Assets	7.9%
Implied Annual Dividend Per Share	2.0%

= LTM Adjusted EBIT / Average (Total Debt$_{2011}$ - Cash$_{2011}$+ Shareholders' Equity$_{2011}$, Total Debt$_{9/30/2012}$ - Cash$_{9/30/2012}$ + Shareholders' Equity$_{9/30/2012}$)
= $725.0 million / (($1,875.0 million - $75.0 million + $1,600.0 million) + ($1,850.0 million - $100.0 million + $1,725.0 million) / 2)

= LTM Adjusted Net Income / Average (Shareholders' Equity$_{2011}$, Shareholders' Equity$_{9/30/2012}$)
= $387.5 million / ($1,600.0 million + $1,725.0 million) / 2

= LTM Adjusted Net Income / Average (Total Assets$_{2011}$,Total Assets$_{9/30/2012}$)
= $387.5 million / ($4,825.0 million + $5,000.0 million) / 2

= (Quarterly Dividend x 4) / Current Share Price
= ($0.25 x 4) / $50.00

a. 21.1%. Return on invested capital is calculated as LTM adjusted EBIT divided by the average of total invested capital (sum of debt and shareholders' equity less cash). ($725.0 million / (($1,875.0 million − $75.0 million + $1,600.0 million) + ($1,850.0 million − $100.0 million + $1,725.0 million) / 2))

b. 23.2%. Return on equity is calculated as LTM adjusted net income divided by average shareholders' equity. (($387.5 million / ($1,725.0 million + $1,600.0 million) / 2)

c. 7.9%. Return on assets is calculated as LTM adjusted net income divided by average assets. ($387.5 million / ($4,825.0 million + $5,000.0 million) / 2)

d. 2.0%. Implied Average Divided Per Share is calculated as the most recent quarterly dividend multiplied by four and divided by the current share price. (($0.25 × 4) / $50.00)

5) Credit statistics

LTM Credit Statistics	
Debt/Total Capitalization	51.7%
Total Debt/EBITDA	2.1x
Net Debt/EBITDA	1.9x
EBITDA/Interest Expense	9.0x
(EBITDA-capex)/Interest Expense	7.0x
EBIT/Interest Expense	7.3x

= Total Debt$_{9/30/2012}$ / (Total Debt$_{9/30/2012}$ + Shareholders' Equity$_{9/30/2012}$)
= $1,850.0 million / ($1,850.0 million + $1,725.0 million)

= Total Debt$_{9/30/2012}$ / LTM Adjusted EBITDA
= $1,850.0 million / $900.0 million

= (Total Debt$_{9/30/2012}$ - Cash$_{9/30/2012}$) / LTM Adjusted EBITDA
= ($1,850.0 million - $100.0 million) / $900.0 million

= LTM Adjusted EBITDA / LTM Interest Expense
= $900.0 million / $100.0 million

= (LTM Adjusted EBITDA - Capex) / LTM Interest Expense
= ($900.0 million - $205.0 million) / $100.0 million

= LTM Adjusted EBIT / LTM Interest Expense
= $725.0 million / $100.0 million

a. 51.7%. Debt-to-total capitalization is calculated as debt divided by total capitalization. ($1,850.0 million / ($1,850.0 million + $1,725.0 million))

b. 2.1x. Total debt-to-EBITDA is calculated as total debt divided by LTM adjusted EBITDA. ($1,850.0 million / $900.0 million)

c. 1.9x. Net debt-to-EBITDA is calculated as net debt (total debt less cash) divided by LTM adjusted EBITDA. (($1,850.0 million – $100.0 million) / $900.0 million)

d. 9.0x. EBITDA-to-interest expense is calculated as LTM adjusted EBITDA divided by LTM interest expense. ($900.0 million / $100.0 million)

e. 7.0x. (EBITDA – capex)-to- interest expense is calculated as LTM adjusted EBITDA less capex divided by LTM interest expense. (($900.0 million – $205.0 million) / $100.0 million)

f. 7.3x. EBIT-to-interest expense is calculated as LTM adjusted EBIT divided by LTM interest expense. ($725.0 million / $100.0 million)

6) Trading multiples

($ in millions, except per share data)

Trading Multiples	LTM 9/30/2012	NFY 2012E	NFY+1 2013E	NFY+2 2014E
EV / Sales	1.4x	1.4x	1.3x	1.2x
Metric	$4,725.0	$5,000.0	$5,350.0	$5,625.0
EV / EBITDA	7.5x	7.1x	6.6x	6.3x
Metric	$900.0	$950.0	$1,025.0	$1,075.0
EV / EBIT	9.3x	8.8x	8.2x	7.8x
Metric	$725.0	$765.0	$825.0	$865.0
P/E	12.9x	11.2x	10.0x	9.1x
Metric	$3.88	$4.45	$5.00	$5.50
FCF Yield	6.3%	7.0%	7.5%	8.3%
Metric	$315.0	$350.0	$375.0	$415.0

= Enterprise Value / LTM Sales
= $6,750.0 million / $4,725.0 million

= Current Share Price / 2014E EPS
= $50.00 / $5.50

= Enterprise Value / 2012E EBITDA
= $6,750.0 million / $950.0 million

= Enterprise Value / 2013E EBIT
= $6,750.0 million / $825.0 million

= 2014E Free Cash Flow / Equity Value
= $415.0 million / $5,000.0 million

a. 1.4x. Enterprise value-to-LTM sales is calculated as enterprise value divided by LTM sales. ($6,750.0 million / $4,750.0 million)

b. 7.1x. Enterprise value-to-NFY EBITDA is calculated as enterprise value divided by 2012E EBITDA. ($6,750.0 million / $950.0 million)

c. 8.2x. Enterprise value-to-NFY+1 EBIT is calculated as enterprise value divided by 2013E EBIT. ($6,750.0 million / $825.0 million)

d. 9.1x. Price/NFY+2 EPS is calculated as the current share price divided by 2014E EPS. ($50.00 / $5.50)

e. 8.3%. FCF Yield (NFY+2 Free cash flow-to-equity value) is calculated as 2014E Free cash flow divided by equity value. ($415.0 million / $5,000.0 million)

7) Growth rates

| = (2013E EPS / 2011 Adjusted EPS) ^ (1 / (2013E - 2011)) - 1 |
| = ($5.00 / $3.40) ^ (1 / 2) - 1 |

| = 2012E FCF / 2011 FCF - 1 |
| = $350.0 million / $300.0 million - 1 |

	Sales	EBITDA	FCF	EPS
Historical				
1-year ('10-'11)	8.4%	5.1%	13.2%	6.4%
2-year CAGR ('09-'11)	9.5%	8.2%	14.2%	11.6%
Estimated				
1-year ('11-'12E)	11.1%	15.2%	16.7%	31.0%
2-year CAGR ('11-'13E)	9.0%	11.5%	11.8%	21.3%

| = 2011 Sales / 2010 Sales - 1 |
| = $4,500.0 million / $4,150.0 million - 1 |

| = (2011 Adjusted EBITDA / 2009 EBITDA) ^ (1 / (2011 - 2009)) - 1 |
| = ($825.0 million / $705.0 million) ^ (1 / 2) - 1 |

a. 8.4%. One year historical sales growth is calculated as 2011A sales divided by 2010A sales, minus one. ($4,500 million / $4,150 million − 1)

b. 8.2%. Two year historical EBITDA CAGR is calculated using the following formula: ((2011A Adjusted EBITDA / 2009A EBITDA) ^ (1 / (2011A − 2009A)) − 1). (($825.0 million / $705.0 million) ^ (1 / 2) − 1)

c. 16.7%. One year estimated FCF growth is calculated as 2012E FCF divided by 2011A FCF, minus one. ($350.0 million / $300.0 million − 1)

d. 21.3%. Two year estimated EPS CAGR is calculated using the following formula: ((2013E EPS / 2011A Adjusted EPS) ^ (1 / (2013E − 2011A)) − 1) (($5.00 / $3.40) ^ (1 / 2) − 1)

8) Benchmarking financial statistics and profitability ratios

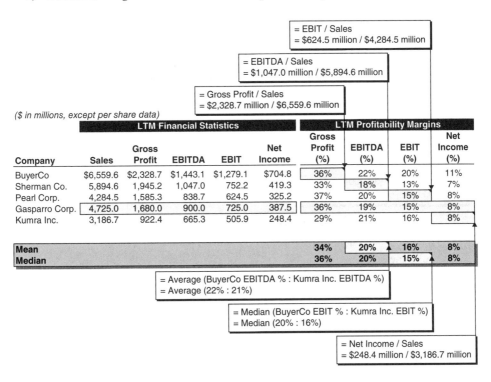

= EBIT / Sales
= $624.5 million / $4,284.5 million

= EBITDA / Sales
= $1,047.0 million / $5,894.6 million

= Gross Profit / Sales
= $2,328.7 million / $6,559.6 million

($ in millions, except per share data)

	LTM Financial Statistics					LTM Profitability Margins			
Company	Sales	Gross Profit	EBITDA	EBIT	Net Income	Gross Profit (%)	EBITDA (%)	EBIT (%)	Net Income (%)
BuyerCo	$6,559.6	$2,328.7	$1,443.1	$1,279.1	$704.8	36%	22%	20%	11%
Sherman Co.	5,894.6	1,945.2	1,047.0	752.2	419.3	33%	18%	13%	7%
Pearl Corp.	4,284.5	1,585.3	838.7	624.5	325.2	37%	20%	15%	8%
Gasparro Corp.	4,725.0	1,680.0	900.0	725.0	387.5	36%	19%	15%	8%
Kumra Inc.	3,186.7	922.4	665.3	505.9	248.4	29%	21%	16%	8%
Mean						34%	20%	16%	8%
Median						36%	20%	15%	8%

= Average (BuyerCo EBITDA % : Kumra Inc. EBITDA %)
= Average (22% : 21%)

= Median (BuyerCo EBIT % : Kumra Inc. EBIT %)
= Median (20% : 16%)

= Net Income / Sales
= $248.4 million / $3,186.7 million

a. 35.5%. Gross profit margin is calculated as gross profit divided by sales. ($2,328.7 million / $6,559.6 million)

b. 17.8%. EBITDA margin is calculated as EBITDA divided by sales. ($1,047.0 million / $5,894.6 million)

c. 14.6%. EBIT margin is calculated as EBIT divided by sales. ($624.5 million / $4,284.5 million)

d. 7.8%. Net income margin is calculated as net income divided by sales. ($248.4 million / $3,186.7 million)

e. 19.9%. The mean EBITDA margin for the comparable companies is calculated by taking the average of the EBITDA margins for the comparable companies

f. 15.3%. The median EBIT margin for the comparable companies is calculated by taking the median of the EBIT margins for the comparable companies

9)　Benchmarking leverage and coverage ratios

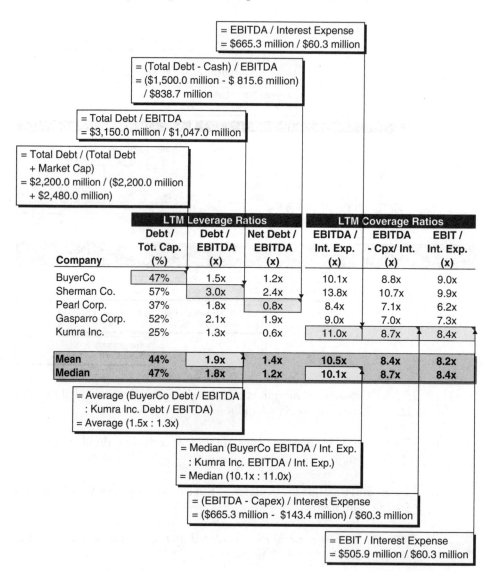

= EBITDA / Interest Expense
= $665.3 million / $60.3 million

= (Total Debt - Cash) / EBITDA
= ($1,500.0 million - $ 815.6 million)
　/ $838.7 million

= Total Debt / EBITDA
= $3,150.0 million / $1,047.0 million

= Total Debt / (Total Debt
　+ Market Cap)
= $2,200.0 million / ($2,200.0 million
　+ $2,480.0 million)

	LTM Leverage Ratios			LTM Coverage Ratios		
Company	Debt / Tot. Cap. (%)	Debt / EBITDA (x)	Net Debt / EBITDA (x)	EBITDA / Int. Exp. (x)	EBITDA - Cpx/ Int. (x)	EBIT / Int. Exp. (x)
BuyerCo	47%	1.5x	1.2x	10.1x	8.8x	9.0x
Sherman Co.	57%	3.0x	2.4x	13.8x	10.7x	9.9x
Pearl Corp.	37%	1.8x	0.8x	8.4x	7.1x	6.2x
Gasparro Corp.	52%	2.1x	1.9x	9.0x	7.0x	7.3x
Kumra Inc.	25%	1.3x	0.6x	11.0x	8.7x	8.4x
Mean	44%	1.9x	1.4x	10.5x	8.4x	8.2x
Median	47%	1.8x	1.2x	10.1x	8.7x	8.4x

= Average (BuyerCo Debt / EBITDA
　: Kumra Inc. Debt / EBITDA)
= Average (1.5x : 1.3x)

= Median (BuyerCo EBITDA / Int. Exp.
　: Kumra Inc. EBITDA / Int. Exp.)
= Median (10.1x : 11.0x)

= (EBITDA - Capex) / Interest Expense
= ($665.3 million - $143.4 million) / $60.3 million

= EBIT / Interest Expense
= $505.9 million / $60.3 million

a.　47.0%. Debt-to-total capital is calculated as total debt divided by debt plus market capitalization. ($2,200.0 million / ($2,200.0 million + $2,480.0 million))

b.　3.0x. Debt-to-EBTIDA is calculated as total debt divided by EBITDA. ($3,150.0 million / $1,047.0 million)

c.　0.8x. Net debt-to-EBITDA is calculated as total debt minus cash divided by EBTIDA. (($1,500.0 million – $ 815.6 million) / $838.7 million)

d. 11.0x. EBITDA-to-interest expense is calculated as EBITDA divided by interest expense. ($665.3 million / $60.3 million)

e. 8.7x. (EBITDA – Capex)-to-interest expense is calculated as EBITDA minus capital expenditures divided by interest expense. (($665.3 million – $143.4 million) / $60.3 million)

f. 8.4x. EBIT-to-interest expense is calculated as EBIT divided by interest expense. ($505.9 million / $60.3 million)

g. 1.9x. The mean Debt-to-EBITDA ratio for the comparable companies is calculated by taking the average of the Debt-to-EBITDA ratios for the comparable companies

h. 10.1x. The median EBITDA-to-interest expense ratio for the comparable companies is calculated by taking the median of the EBITDA-to-interest expense ratios for the comparable companies

10) Comparable companies analysis

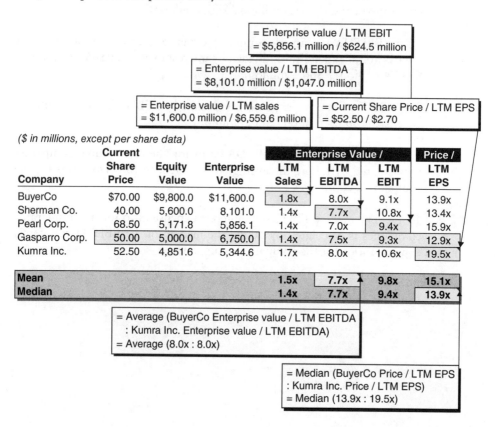

($ in millions, except per share data)

Company	Current Share Price	Equity Value	Enterprise Value	Enterprise Value / LTM Sales	LTM EBITDA	LTM EBIT	Price / LTM EPS
BuyerCo	$70.00	$9,800.0	$11,600.0	1.8x	8.0x	9.1x	13.9x
Sherman Co.	40.00	5,600.0	8,101.0	1.4x	7.7x	10.8x	13.4x
Pearl Corp.	68.50	5,171.8	5,856.1	1.4x	7.0x	9.4x	15.9x
Gasparro Corp.	50.00	5,000.0	6,750.0	1.4x	7.5x	9.3x	12.9x
Kumra Inc.	52.50	4,851.6	5,344.6	1.7x	8.0x	10.6x	19.5x
Mean				**1.5x**	**7.7x**	**9.8x**	**15.1x**
Median				**1.4x**	**7.7x**	**9.4x**	**13.9x**

= Enterprise value / LTM EBIT
= $5,856.1 million / $624.5 million

= Enterprise value / LTM EBITDA
= $8,101.0 million / $1,047.0 million

= Enterprise value / LTM sales
= $11,600.0 million / $6,559.6 million

= Current Share Price / LTM EPS
= $52.50 / $2.70

= Average (BuyerCo Enterprise value / LTM EBITDA
: Kumra Inc. Enterprise value / LTM EBITDA)
= Average (8.0x : 8.0x)

= Median (BuyerCo Price / LTM EPS
: Kumra Inc. Price / LTM EPS)
= Median (13.9x : 19.5x)

a. 1.8x. Enterprise value-to-LTM sales is calculated as enterprise value divided by LTM sales. ($11,600.0 million / $6,559.6 million)

b. 7.7x. Enterprise value-to-LTM EBITDA is calculated as enterprise value divided by LTM EBITDA. ($8,101.0 million / $1,047.0 million)

c. 9.4x. Enterprise value-to-LTM EBIT is calculated as enterprise value divided by LTM EBIT. ($5,856.1 million / $624.5 million)

d. 19.5x. Price-to-LTM EPS is calculated as the current share price divided by LTM EPS. ($52.50 / $2.70)

e. 7.7x. The mean Enterprise value-to-LTM EBITDA multiple for the comparable companies is calculated by taking the average of the Enterprise value-to-LTM EBITDA multiples for the comparable companies

f. 13.9x. The median price-to-LTM EPS multiple for the comparable companies is calculated by taking the median of the price-to-LTM EPS multiples for the comparable companies.

11) Implied valuation ranges using LTM EBITDA

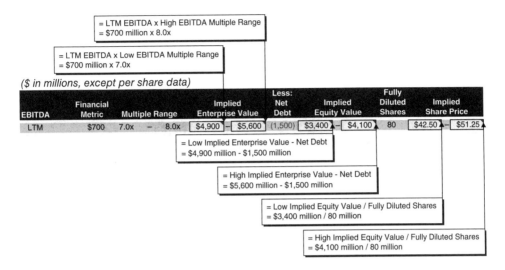

a. $4,900 million. Low implied enterprise value is calculated as LTM EBITDA multiplied by the low EBITDA multiple range. ($700 million × 7.0x)

$5,600 million. High implied enterprise value is calculated as LTM EBITDA multiplied by the high EBITDA multiple range. ($700 million × 8.0x)

b. $3,400 million. Low implied equity value is calculated as low implied enterprise value minus net debt. ($4,900 million − $1,500 million)

$4,100 million. High implied equity value is calculated as high implied enterprise value minus net debt. ($5,600.0 million − $1,500 million)

c. $42.50. Low implied share price is calculated as low implied equity value divided by fully diluted shares. ($3,400 million / 80 million)

$51.25. High implied share price is calculated as high implied equity value divided by fully diluted shares. ($4,100 million / 80 million)

12) Implied valuation range using LTM net income

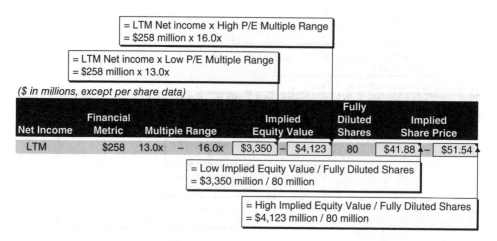

a. $3,350 million. Low implied equity value is calculated as LTM net income multiplied by the low P/E multiple range. ($258 million × 13.0x)

$4,123 million. High implied equity value is calculated as LTM net income multiplied by the high P/E multiple range. ($258 million × 16.0x)

b. $41.88. Low implied share price is calculated as low implied equity value divided by fully diluted shares. ($3,350 million / 80 million)

$51.54. High implied share price is calculated as high implied equity value divided by fully diluted shares. ($4,123 million / 80 million)

13) A. The correct order is:

 I. Select the Universe of Comparable Companies
 II. Locate the Necessary Financial Information
 III. Spread Key Statistics, Ratios, and Trading Multiples
 IV. Benchmark the Comparable Companies
 V. Determine Valuation

14) C. Although all four characteristics can be used to determine the universe of comparable companies, return on investment is a financial characteristic, not a business characteristic

Business Profile
■ Sector
■ Products and Services
■ Customers and End Markets
■ Distribution Channels
■ Geography

15) D. Although all four characteristics can be used to determine the universe of comparable companies, geography is a business characteristic, not a financial characteristic

Financial Profile
■ Size
■ Profitability
■ Growth Profile
■ Return on Investment
■ Credit Profile

16) C. Sector, end markets and distribution channels are key business characteristics to examine when screening for comparable companies

17) B. Profitability, growth profile, and credit profile are key financial characteristics to examine when screening for comparable companies

18) A. A company's end markets refer to the broad underlying markets into which it sells its products and services. For example, a plastics manufacturer may sell into several end markets, including automotive, construction, consumer products, medical devices, and packaging. End markets need to be distinguished from customers. For example, a company may sell into the housing end market, but to retailers or suppliers as opposed to homebuilders.

19) B. Distribution channels are the mediums through which a company sells its products and services to the end user. Companies that sell primarily to the wholesale channel, for example, often have significantly different organizational and cost structures than those selling directly to retailers or end users. Selling to a superstore or value retailer requires a physical infrastructure, sales force, and logistics that may be unnecessary for serving the professional or wholesale channels. Some companies sell at several levels of the distribution chain, such as wholesale, retail, and direct-to-customer.

20) D. In addition to gross profit, EBITDA margin, and EBIT margin, net income margin can also be used to determine the profitability of a company.

21) B. A Schedule 13-D is required when an investor, or group of investors, acquires more than 5% of a company's shares. A Schedule 13-D does not contain relevant financial information for comparable companies.

22) B. Fully diluted shares outstanding are calculated as basic shares outstanding + "in-the-money" options and warrants + "in-the-money" convertible securities. Only "in-the-money" options, warrants and convertible securities are included in the calculation for comparable companies analysis.

23) A. The incremental shares represented by a company's "in-the-money" options and warrants are calculated in accordance with the treasury stock method (TSM). "In-the-money" convertible and equity-linked securities are calculated in accordance with the "if-converted method" or net share settlement (NSS), where appropriate.

24) A. Equity value ("market capitalization") is the value represented by a given company's basic shares outstanding plus "in-the-money" stock options warrants, and convertible securities—collectively, "fully diluted shares outstanding." Enterprise value ("total enterprise value" or "firm value") is the sum of all ownership interests in a company and claims on its assets from both debt and equity holders. It is defined as equity value + total debt + preferred stock + noncontrolling interest − cash and cash equivalents.

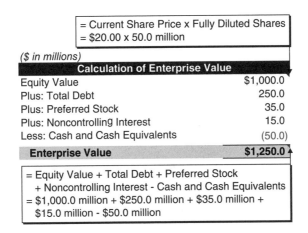

= Current Share Price x Fully Diluted Shares
= $20.00 x 50.0 million

($ in millions)

Calculation of Enterprise Value	
Equity Value	$1,000.0
Plus: Total Debt	250.0
Plus: Preferred Stock	35.0
Plus: Noncontrolling Interest	15.0
Less: Cash and Cash Equivalents	(50.0)
Enterprise Value	**$1,250.0**

= Equity Value + Total Debt + Preferred Stock
  + Noncontrolling Interest - Cash and Cash Equivalents
= $1,000.0 million + $250.0 million + $35.0 million +
  $15.0 million - $50.0 million

25) C. As shown below, the 20 million options are in-the-money as the exercise price of $10.00 is lower than the current share price of $25.00. This means that the holders of the options have the right to buy the company's shares at $10.00 and sell them at $25.00, thereby realizing the $15.00 differential. Under the TSM, it is assumed that the $10.00 of potential proceeds received by the company is used to repurchase shares that are currently trading at $25.00. Therefore, the number of shares repurchased is 8 million. To calculate net new shares, the 8 million shares repurchased are subtracted from the 20 million options, resulting in 12 million. These new shares are added to the company's basic shares outstanding to derive fully diluted shares of 212.0 million.

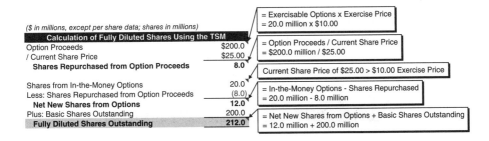

($ in millions, except per share data; shares in millions)

Calculation of Fully Diluted Shares Using the TSM	
Option Proceeds	$200.0
/ Current Share Price	$25.00
Shares Repurchased from Option Proceeds	**8.0**
Shares from In-the-Money Options	20.0
Less: Shares Repurchased from Option Proceeds	(8.0)
Net New Shares from Options	**12.0**
Plus: Basic Shares Outstanding	200.0
Fully Diluted Shares Outstanding	**212.0**

= Exercisable Options x Exercise Price
= 20.0 million x $10.00

= Option Proceeds / Current Share Price
= $200.0 million / $25.00

Current Share Price of $25.00 > $10.00 Exercise Price

= In-the-Money Options - Shares Repurchased
= 20.0 million - 8.0 million

= Net New Shares from Options + Basic Shares Outstanding
= 12.0 million + 200.0 million

26)   C. See calculation below:

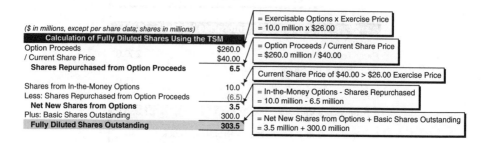

($ in millions, except per share data; shares in millions)	
Calculation of Fully Diluted Shares Using the TSM	
Option Proceeds	$260.0
/ Current Share Price	$40.00
Shares Repurchased from Option Proceeds	6.5
Shares from In-the-Money Options	10.0
Less: Shares Repurchased from Option Proceeds	(6.5)
Net New Shares from Options	3.5
Plus: Basic Shares Outstanding	300.0
Fully Diluted Shares Outstanding	303.5

- = Exercisable Options x Exercise Price
  = 10.0 million x $26.00
- = Option Proceeds / Current Share Price
  = $260.0 million / $40.00
- Current Share Price of $40.00 > $26.00 Exercise Price
- = In-the-Money Options - Shares Repurchased
  = 10.0 million - 6.5 million
- = Net New Shares from Options + Basic Shares Outstanding
  = 3.5 million + 300.0 million

27)   D. Net debt is subtracted from enterprise value to calculate implied equity value.

28)   A. The most dilutive scenario would be to use all outstanding options and warrants.

29)   C. Stock options become eligible to be converted into shares of common stock once their vesting period expires ("exercisable").

30)   C. As the company's current share price of $45.00 is greater than the conversion price of $30.00, the $300 million convert is in-the-money. Therefore, the convert's amount outstanding is divided by the conversion price to calculate new shares of 10 million ($300 million / $30.00). The new shares from conversion are then added to the company's basic shares outstanding of 250 million to calculate fully diluted shares outstanding of 260 million.

- = Amount Outstanding / Converstion Price
  = $300.0 million / $30.00

($ in millions, except per share data; shares in millions)	
If-Converted Method	
Amount Outstanding	$300.0
/ Conversion Price	$30.00
Incremental Shares	10.0
Plus: Basic Shares Outstanding	250.0
Fully Diluted Shares Outstanding	260.0

- = New Shares from Conversion + Basic Shares Outstanding
  = 10.0 million + 250.0 million

31) D. See calculation below:

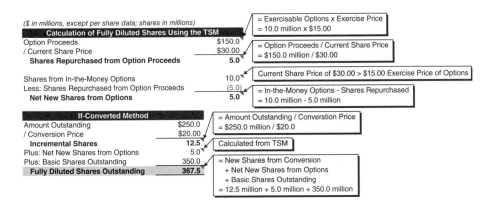

32) C. See calculation below:

($ in millions, except per share data; shares in millions	
If-Converted Method	
Amount Outstanding	$225.0
/ Conversion Price	$22.50
Incremental Shares	**10.0**

33) A. The net share settlement method ("NSS") calculation is performed by first multiplying the number of underlying shares in the convert of 10 million by the company's current share price of $30.00 to determine the implied conversion value of $300 million. The $75 million spread between the conversion value and par ($300 million – $225 million) is then divided by the current share price to determine the number of incremental shares from conversion of 2.5 million ($75 million / $30.00).

($ in millions, except per share data; shares in millions)

Net Share Settlement	
Amount Outstanding	$225.0
/ Conversion Price	$22.50
Incremental Shares	**10.0**
x Current Share Price	$30.00
Total Conversion Value	**$300.0**
Less: Par Value of Amount Outstanding	(225.0)
Excess Over Par Value	**$75.0**
/ Current Share Price	$30.00
Incremental Shares – NSS	**2.5**

= Excess Over Par Value / Current Share Price
= $75.0 million / $30.00

= Total Conversion Value - Par Value of Amt. Out.
= $300.0 million - $225.0 million

= Incremental Shares x Current Share Price
= 10.0 million x $30.00

= Amount Outstanding / Conversion Price
= $225.0 million / $22.50

34) B. The formula for enterprise value is equity value + total debt + preferred stock + noncontrolling interest – cash.

35) A. As enterprise value is independent of capital structure, it remains constant regardless of changes in capital structure.

36) If a company issues equity and uses the proceeds to repay debt, the incremental equity value is offset by the decrease in debt on a dollar-for-dollar basis.

($ in millions)

Issuance of Equity to Repay Debt				
	Actual	Adjustments		Pro forma
	2012	+	-	2012
Equity Value	$1,200.0	200.0		$1,400.0
Plus: Total Debt	750.0		(200.0)	550.0
Plus: Preferred Stock	100.0			100.0
Plus: Minority Interest	50.0			50.0
Less: Cash and Cash Equivalents	(100.0)			(100.0)
Enterprise Value	**$2,000.0**			**$2,000.0**

37) B. The gross profit margin for Company B is 45.0% while Company A has a gross profit margin of 37.5%. The calculation for gross profit margin is shown below.

$$\text{Gross Profit Margin} = \frac{\text{Gross Profit (Sales} - \text{COGS)}}{\text{Sales}}$$

38) A. See calculation below:

Fiscal Year Ending December 31,							
	2010A	**2011A**	**2012A**	**CAGR ('10 - '12)**	**2013E**	**2014E**	**CAGR ('12 - '14)**
Diluted EPS	$1.35	$1.60	$1.80	15.5%	$2.00	$2.20	10.6%
% growth		*18.5%*	*12.5%*		*11.1%*	*10.0%*	

= (Ending Value / Beginning Value) ^ (1 / Ending Year - Beginning Year) - 1
= ($1.80 / $1.35) ^ (1 / (2012 - 2010)) - 1

= (Ending Value / Beginning Value) ^ (1 / Ending Year - Beginning Year) - 1
= ($1.80 / $1.35) ^ (1 / (2012 - 2010)) - 1

39) C. In assessing a company's growth profile, historical and estimated future growth rates for various financial statistics (e.g., sales, EBITDA, and earnings per share (EPS)) are examined at selected intervals. EBITDA margin, which measures a company's operating profitability, is not used to measure growth.

40) B. As shown below, return on invested capital (ROIC) utilizes a pre-interest earnings statistic in the numerator, such as EBIT, and a metric that captures both debt and equity in the denominator.

$$\text{ROIC} = \frac{\text{EBIT}}{\text{Average Net Debt} + \text{Equity}}$$

41) C. Return on equity (ROE) incorporates an earnings metric net of interest expense, such as net income, in the numerator and average shareholders' equity in the denominator. The calculation for ROE is shown below.

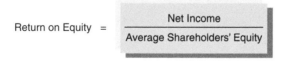

$$\text{Return on Equity} = \frac{\text{Net Income}}{\text{Average Shareholders' Equity}}$$

42)   C. As shown below, return on assets (ROA) utilizes net income in the numerator and average total assets in the denominator.

$$\text{Return on Assets} = \frac{\text{Net Income}}{\text{Average Total Assets}}$$

43)   A. Debt-to-total capitalization measures a company's debt as a percentage of its total capitalization (debt + preferred stock + noncontrolling interest + equity). The formula for debt-to-total capitalization is shown below.

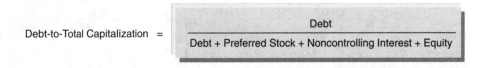

$$\text{Debt-to-Total Capitalization} = \frac{\text{Debt}}{\text{Debt} + \text{Preferred Stock} + \text{Noncontrolling Interest} + \text{Equity}}$$

44)   A. The numerator in an interest coverage ratio can be comprised of EBITDA, (EBITDA – Capex), or EBIT, which are all financial statistics representing an operating cash flow metric. Net income does not fit this characteristic because it is net of interest expense and taxes.

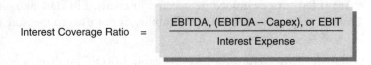

$$\text{Interest Coverage Ratio} = \frac{\text{EBITDA, (EBITDA – Capex), or EBIT}}{\text{Interest Expense}}$$

45) B. As the graphic below shows, Aaa, Aa1, and Aa2 are credit ratings assigned by Moody's.

	Moody's	S&P	Fitch	Definition
Investment Grade	**Aaa**	AAA	AAA	Highest Quality
	Aa1	AA+	AA+	
	Aa2	AA	AA	Very High Quality
	Aa3	AA–	AA–	
	A1	A+	A+	
	A2	A	A	High Quality
	A3	A–	A–	
	Baa1	BBB+	BBB+	
	Baa2	BBB	BBB	Medium Grade
	Baa3	BBB–	BBB–	
Non-Investment Grade	Ba1	BB+	BB+	
	Ba2	BB	BB	Speculative
	Ba3	BB–	BB–	
	B1	B+	B+	
	B2	B	B	Highly Speculative
	B3	B–	B–	
	Caa1	CCC+	CCC+	
	Caa2	CCC	CCC	Substantial Risk
	Caa3	CCC–	CCC–	
	Ca	CC	CC	
	C	C	C	Extremely Speculative /
	–	D	D	Default

46) D. BBB- is investment grade (see table in question #45).

47) A. The equivalent of B+ is B1 (see table in question #45).

48) D. LTM 9/30/2012 sales are calculated by taking $2,250.0 million (2011 FY sales from 10-K), adding $1,600.0 million (2012 YTD sales from 10-Q), and then subtracting $1,450.0 million (2011 YTD sales from 10-Q).

LTM = Prior Fiscal Year + Current Stub − Prior Stub

($ in millions)

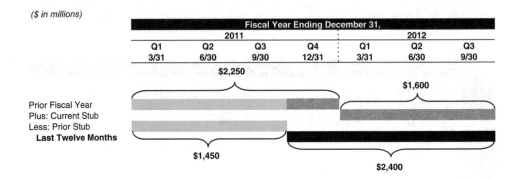

49) B. In this case, the most recent quarter is the fourth quarter of the company's fiscal year. Therefore, there is no LTM calculation as the full prior fiscal year (as reported) serves as the LTM period.

50) C. To calendarize 4/30/2012 sales, take year end 4/30/2012 sales and multiply the data by 4/12, the numerator pertaining to the month # in which the company's fiscal year ends. Next, take 4/30/2013 projected sales, and multiply the data by 8/12, the numerator pertaining to one minus the month # in which the company's fiscal year ends. The sum of these two formulas is estimated 12/31/2012 sales.

Next Calendar Year (CY) Sales $= \dfrac{(\text{Month \#}) \times (\text{FYA Sales})}{12} + \dfrac{(12 - \text{Month \#}) \times (\text{NFY Sales})}{12}$

Note: "Month #" refers to the month in which the company's fiscal year ends (e.g. the Month # for a company with a fiscal year ending April 30 would be 4). FYA = fiscal year actual and NFY = next fiscal year.

($ in millions)

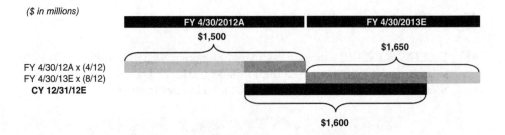

51) B. See calculation below

($ in millions, except per share data)

Income Statement	Reported 2012	Adjustments +	Adjustments -	Adjusted 2012	
Sales	$1,000.0			$1,000.0	
Cost of Goods Sold	625.0		(5.0)	620.0	Inventory write-down
Gross Profit	$375.0			$380.0	
Selling, General & Administrative	230.0			230.0	
Restructuring Charges	10.0		(10.0)	-	
Operating Income (EBIT)	$135.0			$150.0	
Interest Expense	35.0			35.0	
Pre-tax Income	$100.0			$115.0	
Income Taxes @ 40%	40.0	6.0		46.0	= (Inventory write-down + Restructuring charge) x Marginal Tax Rate
Net Income	$60.0			$69.0	= ($5 million + $10 million) x 40%

Operating Income (EBIT)	$135.0	15.0		$150.0	
Depreciation & Amortization	50.0			50.0	
EBITDA	$185.0			$200.0	

Weighted Avg. Diluted Shares	30.0		30.0
Diluted EPS	$2.00		$2.30

$15 million add-back of total non-recurring items

52) A. P/E is equal to equity value/net income.

$$\frac{\text{Share Price}}{\text{Diluted EPS}} \qquad \frac{\text{Equity Value}}{\text{Net Income}}$$

53) C. For enterprise value multiples, the denominator employs a financial statistic that flows to both debt and equity holders, such as sales, EBITDA, and EBIT. Thus, Enterprise value/net income is incorrect because net income only flows to equity holders as it is net of interest expense.

54) A. Equity value-to-EBITDA is incorrect because its numerator, equity value, corresponds to a financial statistic that flows only to equity holders, such as net income or EPS. EBITDA flows to both equity and debt holders.

55) B. The balance sheet shows the cumulative amount of noncontrolling interest.

56) B. Enterprise value-to-EBITDA and Price-to-earnings (P/E) are the two most generic and widely used valuation multiples.

57) Similar companies provide a highly relevant reference point for valuing a given target due to the fact that they share key business and financial characteristics, performance drivers, and risks.

58) One of the companies could have higher profit margins, higher levels of projected growth, or less leverage; while the other company could have experienced management turnover, missed earnings estimates, or business disruptions.

59) Moderate to low leverage. Such a company has a lower risk of financial distress, coupled with a greater ability to grow both organically and through acquisitions.

60) Certain sub-groups are typically more appropriate than the entire universe for framing valuation (e.g., based on business model, size, and geography). This tiering requires a sufficient number of comparable companies to justify categorization.

61) See below

10-K	Annual report
10-Q	Quarterly report
8-K	Current report
DEF14A	Proxy statement

62) See below

Enterprise value/reserves	Metals & mining
Enterprise value/EBITDAR	Retail
Enterprise value/subscriber	Media
Price/Book	Financial Institutions

63) Benefits of using comparable companies:

▪ *Market-based* – information used to derive valuation for the target is based on actual public market data, thereby reflecting the market's growth and risk expectations, as well as overall sentiment

▪ *Relativity* – easily measurable and comparable versus other companies

▪ *Quick and convenient* – valuation can be determined on the basis of a few easy-to-calculate inputs

▪ *Current* – valuation is based on prevailing market data, which can be updated on a daily (or intraday) basis

64) Considerations when using comparable companies::

▪ *Market-based* – valuation that is completely market-based can be skewed during periods of irrational exuberance or bearishness

▪ *Absence of relevant comparables* – "pure play" comparables may be difficult to identify or even non-existent, especially if the target operates in a niche sector, in which case the valuation implied by trading comps may be less meaningful

▪ *Potential disconnect from cash flow* – valuation based on prevailing market conditions or expectations may have significant disconnect from the valuation implied by a company's projected cash flow generation (e.g., DCF analysis)

▪ *Company-specific issues* – valuation of the target is based on the valuation of other companies, which may fail to capture target-specific strengths, weaknesses, opportunities, and risks

CHAPTER 2

Precedent Transactions Analysis

1) Using the information provided for Rosenbaum Industries, complete the questions regarding fully diluted shares outstanding

General Information	
Target	**Rosenbaum Industries**
Ticker	JNR
Fiscal Year End	Dec-31
Marginal Tax Rate	*38.0%*
Acquirer	**Pearl Corp.**
Ticker	PRL
Fiscal Year End	Dec-31
Date Announced	11/2/2012
Date Effective	Pending
Transaction Type	Public / Public
Purchase Consideration	Cash

(shares in millions)

Assumptions	
Offer Price per Share	$20.00
Basic Shares Outstanding	123.00

Options/Warrants		
Tranche	**Number of Shares**	**Exercise Price**
Tranche 1	1.500	$5.00
Tranche 2	1.250	$10.00
Tranche 3	1.000	$15.00

a. Calculate Rosenbaum Industries' in-the-money options/warrants

_____

b. Calculate total proceeds from in-the-money options/warrants

_____

    c. Calculate net new shares from the options/warrants

_____

    d. Calculate fully diluted shares outstanding

_____

2) Using the prior answers and information, as well as the assumptions below, calculate Rosenbaum Industries' equity value and enterprise value

($ in millions)	
Assumptions	
Total Debt	$1,375.0
Cash and Cash Equivalents	50.0

    a. Calculate equity value

_____

    b. Calculate enterprise value

_____

3) Using the information provided for Rosenbaum Industries, complete the questions regarding non-recurring items

Non-recurring Item

$25.0 million pre-tax payment in regards to a litigation settlement in Q4 2011

($ in millions, except per share data)

Reported Income Statement

	FYE 12/31/2011	Prior Stub 9/30/2011	Current Stub 9/30/2012	LTM 9/30/2012
Sales	$2,250.0	$1,687.5	$1,822.5	$2,385.0
COGS	1,500.0	1,125.0	1,215.0	1,590.0
Gross Profit	$750.0	$562.5	$607.5	$795.0
SG&A	450.0	337.5	364.5	477.0
Other (Income)/Expense	-	-	-	-
EBIT	$300.0	$225.0	$243.0	$318.0
Interest Expense	100.0	75.0	75.0	100.0
Pre-tax Income	$200.0	$150.0	$168.0	$218.0
Income Taxes	76.0	57.0	63.8	82.8
Noncontrolling Interest	-	-	-	-
Preferred Dividends	-	-	-	-
Net Income	$124.0	$93.0	$104.2	$135.2
Effective Tax Rate	*38.0%*	*38.0%*	*38.0%*	*38.0%*
Weighted Avg. Diluted Shares	125.0	125.0	125.0	125.0
Diluted EPS	$0.99	$0.74	$0.83	$1.08

Cash Flow Statement Data

	FYE 12/31/2011	Prior Stub 9/30/2011	Current Stub 9/30/2012	LTM 9/30/2012
Depreciation & Amortization	100.0	75.0	82.0	107.0
% sales	*4.4%*	*4.4%*	*4.5%*	*4.5%*
Capital Expenditures	105.0	75.0	85.0	115.0
% sales	*4.7%*	*4.4%*	*4.7%*	*4.8%*

a. Calculate adjusted gross profit for Rosenbaum Industries assuming the $25.0 million litigation settlement is not a part of COGS

b. Calculate adjusted LTM EBIT, assuming the $25.0 million litigation settlement was included in reported EBIT

c. Calculate adjusted LTM EBITDA

_____

d. Calculate adjusted LTM net income

_____

4) Using the adjusted financials, as well as all other prior answers and information, calculate the transaction multiples for Rosenbaum Industries

($ in millions, except per share data)

LTM Transaction Multiples	
EV/Sales	A)
Metric	
EV/EBITDA	B)
Metric	
EV/EBIT	C)
Metric	
P/E	D)
Metric	

a. Calculate Rosenbaum Industries' enterprise value-to-sales

_____

b. Calculate enterprise value-to-EBITDA

_____

c. Calculate enterprise value-to-EBIT

_____

d. Calculate the P/E ratio

_____

5) Using the prior answers and information, as well as the assumptions below, complete the questions regarding the premiums paid for Rosenbaum Industries

Share Price	
1 Day Prior to Transaction Announcement	$17.39
1 Day Prior to Unaffected Share Price	14.81
7 Days Prior to Unaffected Share Price	15.04
30 Days Prior to Unaffected Share Price	14.60

    a. Calculate the premium paid for Rosenbaum Industries based on the day prior to the transaction announcement

    b. Calculate the premium paid based on one day prior to the unaffected share price

    c. Calculate the premium paid based on seven days prior to the unaffected share price

    d. Calculate the premium paid based on 30 days prior to the unaffected share price

6) Using the prior answers and information, as well as the assumptions below, calculate equity value and enterprise value for the precedent transactions

($ in millions, except per share data; shares in millions)

Financial Data

Target	Offer Price	Fully Diluted Shares	Total Debt	Total Cash
Schneider & Co.	37.25	135.5	1,250.0	125.0
Ackerman Industries	95.00	93.1	1,250.0	100.0

Acquirer	Target	Equity Value	Enterprise Value
Pearl Corp.	Rosenbaum Industries		
Goodson Corp.	Schneider & Co.	A)	$6,173.8
Domanski Capital	Ackerman Industries	$8,845.0	B)

a. Calculate Schneider & Co.'s equity value

_____

b. Calculate Ackerman Industries' enterprise value

_____

7. Using the prior answers and information, as well as the assumptions below, calculate the transaction multiples for the precedent transactions

($ in millions)

LTM Financial Data			
Target	**Sales**	**EBITDA**	**EBIT**
Schneider & Co.	$4,284.5	$764.4	$598.4
Ackerman Industries	5,940.6	1,247.5	980.2
Whalen Inc.	700.0	180.0	140.0

		Enterprise Value /		
Acquirer	**Target**	**LTM Sales**	**LTM EBITDA**	**LTM EBIT**
Pearl Corp.	Rosenbaum Industries			
Goodson Corp.	Schneider & Co.	A)	8.1x	10.3x
Domanski Capital	Ackerman Industries	1.7x	B)	10.2x
The Hochberg Group	Whalen Inc.	1.9x	7.5x	C)
Mean		**1.7x**	**D)**	**10.3x**
Median		**1.6x**	**8.0x**	**E)**
High		**1.9x**	**F)**	**11.2x**
Low		**1.4x**	**7.5x**	**G)**

a. Calculate Schneider & Co.'s enterprise value-to-sales

b. Calculate Ackerman Industries' enterprise value-to-EBITDA

c. Calculate Whalen Inc.'s enterprise value-to-EBIT

d. Calculate the mean enterprise value-to-EBITDA multiple

e. Calculate the median enterprise value-to-EBIT multiple

 f. What is the highest enterprise value-to-EBITDA multiple?

---

 g. What is the lowest enterprise value-to-EBIT multiple?

---

8) Which of the following is NOT a traditional source when creating an initial list of comparable acquisitions?

 A. M&A databases
 B. Target's M&A history
 C. Credit reports
 D. Fairness opinions for recent transactions in the target's sector

9) Which question(s) would a banker typically ask to better understand the context of an M&A deal?

 I. Was the acquirer a strategic buyer or financial sponsor?
 II. Was the nature of the deal friendly or hostile?
 III. Was the target sold through an auction process or negotiated sale?
 IV. What were the buyer's and seller's motivations for the transaction?

 A. I and IV
 B. II and III
 C. III and IV
 D. I, II, III, and IV

10) Why can a strategic buyer often pay more for a target than a financial sponsor?

 I. Synergies
 II. Lower cost of capital
 III. Longer time/investment horizons
 IV. Lower return thresholds

 A. II and III
 B. III and IV
 C. I, III, and IV
 D. I, II, III, and IV

11) What are the most generic and widely-used multiples in precedent transactions?

    I. Enterprise value-to-net income
    II. Enterprise value-to-LTM EBITDA
    III. Offer price-to-LTM diluted EPS
    IV. Offer price-to-LTM EBITDA

    A. II and III
    B. III and IV
    C. I, II, and III
    D. I, II, III, and IV

12) In addition to a high purchase price, what other factors are important to the seller in assessing the value of a proposed bid?

    I. Speed of execution
    II. Date of management presentation
    III. Certainty of completion
    IV. Regulatory approvals needed

    A. II and III
    B. II and IV
    C. I, II, and IV
    D. I, III, and IV

13) Which of following is NOT contained in a merger proxy?

    A. Terms of transaction
    B. Description of the financial analysis underlying the fairness opinion
    C. Definitive purchase/sale agreement
    D. Target's customer list

14) Under what SEC/EDGAR code is a proxy statement filed in connection with a business combination?

    A. Schedule TO
    B. 14D-9
    C. DEFM14A
    D. 13E-3

15) Which of the following SEC filings is filed when an affiliate of the target company is part of the buyout group?

    A. PREM14A
    B. 14D-9
    C. DEFM14A
    D. 13E-3

16) A target has _____ days to respond to a tender offer and file a _____ .

    A. 10; 10-Q
    B. 10; Schedule 14D-9
    C. 15; 10-Q
    D. 15; Schedule TO

17) How many days is a private acquirer given to file an 8-K after a deal's announcement?

    A. 4
    B. 10
    C. 12
    D. Not required

18) Which of the following are purchase consideration options in an M&A transaction?

    I. Cash
    II. Synergies
    III. Taxes
    IV. Stock

    A. I and III
    B. I and IV
    C. II and IV
    D. I, II, III, and IV

19) What is "scarcity value" as it relates to M&A?

    A. Few targets available of strategic importance to a buyer
    B. Target has scarce resources to grow
    C. Target with low multiple
    D. Target with low revenue

20) Which exchange ratio is most common in a stock-for-stock transaction?

    A. Linear
    B. Floating
    C. Fixed
    D. Non-Floating

21) Which of the following are examples of synergies?

    I. Closing of overlapping facilities
    II. Cost savings from headcount reduction
    III. Hiring a new brand marketing team
    IV. Loss of sales due to overlapping customers

    A. I and II
    B. I and III
    C. III and IV
    D. I, II, III, and IV

22) What factors should be considered when selecting precedent transactions?

    I. CEO compensation
    II. Financial characteristics (e.g., growth rates and margins)
    III. Timing
    IV. Size of companies

    A. II and IV
    B. I, II, and IV
    C. II, III, and IV
    D. I, II, III, and IV

23) What is the exchange ratio if an acquirer agrees to exchange 0.5 shares of its stock for every 2 shares of the target's stock?

    A. 0.25
    B. 0.45
    C. 2.0
    D. 4.0

24) Use the information below to determine the implied equity value for the target

(shares in millions)	
Assumptions	
Acquirer's Share Price	$20.00
Target's Fully Diluted Shares Outstanding	200.0
Exchange Ratio	0.25

    A. $1,000 million
    B. $1,200 million
    C. $1,250 million
    D. $1,275 million

25) Assuming a fixed exchange ratio, draw and label the following two lines on the graph below

    ■ Shares received
    ■ Value to target

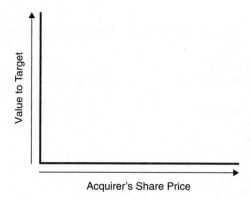

26) Assuming a floating exchange ratio, draw and label the following two lines on the graph below

- Shares received
- Value to target

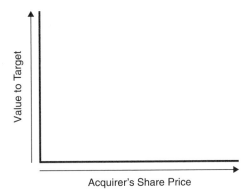

27) Assuming no structural protections for the acquirer, in which structure does the acquirer assume the full risk of a decline in its share price?

A. Fixed
B. Floating
C. Both
D. Neither

28) When is a floating exchange offer most commonly used?

A. Acquirer is significantly larger than target
B. Target is significantly larger than acquirer
C. Target is public
D. Acquirer is public

Use the information below to answer the next two questions

($ in millions, except per share data; shares in millions)	
Assumptions	
Unaffected Share Price	$25.00
Premium Paid	30.0%
Fully Diluted Shares Outstanding	150.0
Total Debt	$1,500.0
Preferred Stock	125.0
Noncontrolling Interest	100.0
Cash	150.0

29) Calculate the target offer value

  A. $3,750 million
  B. $4,500 million
  C. $4,875 million
  D. $5,000 million

30) Calculate the target enterprise value

  A. $4,875 million
  B. $5,875 million
  C. $6,375 million
  D. $6,450 million

31) Calculate the implied premium paid assuming the target has an unaffected share price of $50.00 and the offer price is $67.50 per share

  A. 20%
  B. 25%
  C. 30%
  D. 35%

32) Using the data below, calculate enterprise value-to-EBITDA with and without synergies

($ in millions)

Assumptions	
Enterprise Value	$1,200.0
LTM Revenue	700.0
LTM EBITDA	150.0
Synergies	25.0

    A. 8.0x and 6.9x
    B. 8.0x and 9.6x
    C. 11.7x and 10.0x
    D. 11.7x and 12.3x

33) Why is "time lag" a potential weakness when using precedent transactions?

    A. If the target company in an M&A transaction had a fiscal year ending April 30, it is difficult to include them in the group
    B. Precedent transactions, by definition, took place in the past and it is possible that they do not reflect prevailing market conditions
    C. It takes a long time to spread precedent transactions
    D. Certain precedent transactions were completed in a shorter time period than other deals

34) What are the primary types of synergies?

    I. Revenue
    II. Transaction
    III. Cost
    IV. Time

    A. I and II
    B. I and III
    C. III and IV
    D. I, II, and III

35) Which of the following is NOT a potential weakness of precedent transactions?

    A. Time lag
    B. Scarcity of comparable acquisitions
    C. Locating transaction information
    D. Relativity

36) Select ALL that apply. Which of the following are useful strategies for locating comparable acquisitions?

   I. Search M&A databases
   II. Examine the target's M&A history
   III. Search through merger proxies of comparable acquisitions
   IV. Examine the M&A history of the target's universe of comparable companies

   A. I and II
   B. I, II, and IV
   C. II, III, and IV
   D. I, II, III, and IV

Use the information below to answer the next six questions

(*$ in millions, except per share data; shares in millions*)	
Assumptions	
Office Price Per Share	$15.00
Acquirer Share Price	$30.00
Unaffected Target Share Price	$12.50
Target Basic Shares Outstanding	250.0
Outstanding Options	10.0
Exercise Price	$10.00
Target LTM Revenue	$4,500.0
Target LTM EBITDA	650.0
Target Net Debt	1,000.0

37) Assuming a stock-for-stock transaction, determine the exchange ratio

   A. 0.50
   B. 0.75
   C. 1.1
   D. 2.0

38) What is the premium paid for the target?

   A. 15.0%
   B. 17.0%
   C. 20.0%
   D. 25.0%

39) Calculate the target's fully diluted shares outstanding in accordance with the treasury stock method

   A. 253.3 million
   B. 350.0 million
   C. 416.7 million
   D. 420.3 million

40) Calculate the target's offer value and enterprise value

   A. $3,800 million and $4,800 million
   B. $4,250 million and $5,250 million
   C. $4,750 million and $5,150 million
   D. $5,250 million and $6,250 million

41) Calculate the target's LTM enterprise value-to-EBITDA

   A. 9.0x
   B. 8.4x
   C. 6.4x
   D. 7.4x

42) Calculate the target's LTM enterprise value-to-sales

   A. 1.1x
   B. 1.3x
   C. 1.5x
   D. 2.0x

43) What is the premise behind precedent transactions analysis?

   _____

   _____

   _____

   _____

44) What are the key considerations to examine when screening for comparable acquisitions?

_____

_____

_____

_____

45) Traditionally, have strategic buyers or financial sponsors been able to pay higher purchase prices, and why?

_____

_____

_____

_____

46) Provide examples of how buyer and seller motivations play an important role in interpreting purchase price

_____

_____

_____

_____

47) How might a hostile transaction affect the multiple paid?

_____

_____

_____

_____

48) On which share price(s) is the premiums paid analysis based?

49) When might the day prior to the actual transaction announcement not serve as the appropriate benchmark for establishing the "unaffected" share price?

50) In which type of M&A scenario are synergies most common, and why?

51) Why do public acquirers typically announce expected synergies?

52) What is premiums paid analysis in precedent transactions and what share price should be used in the analysis?

53) Why are transaction multiples in precedent transactions analysis calculated on the basis of LTM financial statistics?

54) In performing a comprehensive valuation of a given target, would precedent transactions be expected to be toward the high end, low end, or middle end of the range?

55) Why do precedent transactions tend to provide higher multiple ranges than comparable companies?

56) When could the valuation range derived from comparable companies be higher than that derived from precedent transactions?

_____

_____

_____

_____

57) What are some of the benefits of using precedent transactions analysis?

_____

_____

_____

_____

58) What are some of the considerations when using precedent transactions analysis?

_____

_____

_____

_____

1) Calculation of fully diluted shares outstanding

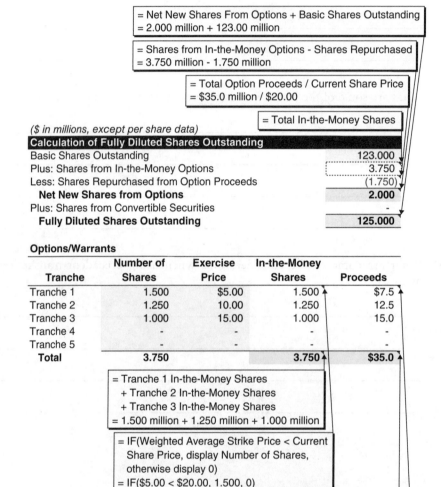

= Net New Shares From Options + Basic Shares Outstanding
= 2.000 million + 123.00 million

= Shares from In-the-Money Options - Shares Repurchased
= 3.750 million - 1.750 million

= Total Option Proceeds / Current Share Price
= $35.0 million / $20.00

= Total In-the-Money Shares

($ in millions, except per share data)

Calculation of Fully Diluted Shares Outstanding	
Basic Shares Outstanding	123.000
Plus: Shares from In-the-Money Options	3.750
Less: Shares Repurchased from Option Proceeds	(1.750)
Net New Shares from Options	**2.000**
Plus: Shares from Convertible Securities	-
Fully Diluted Shares Outstanding	**125.000**

Options/Warrants

Tranche	Number of Shares	Exercise Price	In-the-Money Shares	Proceeds
Tranche 1	1.500	$5.00	1.500	$7.5
Tranche 2	1.250	10.00	1.250	12.5
Tranche 3	1.000	15.00	1.000	15.0
Tranche 4	-	-	-	-
Tranche 5	-	-	-	-
Total	**3.750**		**3.750**	**$35.0**

= Tranche 1 In-the-Money Shares
+ Tranche 2 In-the-Money Shares
+ Tranche 3 In-the-Money Shares
= 1.500 million + 1.250 million + 1.000 million

= IF(Weighted Average Strike Price < Current
Share Price, display Number of Shares,
otherwise display 0)
= IF($5.00 < $20.00, 1.500, 0)

= Tranche 1 In-the-Money Proceeds
+ Tranche 2 In-the-Money Proceeds
+ Tranche 3 In-the-Money Proceeds
= $7.5 million + $12.5 million + $15.0 million

= IF(In-the-Money Shares > 0, then
In-the-Money Shares x Weighted Average
Strike Price, otherwise display 0)
= IF(1.500 > 0, 1.500 x $5.00, 0)

    a. 3.75 million. The total number of Rosenbaum Industries' in-the-money options/warrants is calculated by adding the in-the-money shares from the tranches that have an exercise price lower than the current share price of $20.00. (1.500 million shares + 1.250 million shares + 1.000 million shares)

b. $35.0 million. The total proceeds from in-the-money options/warrants is calculated by adding the proceeds from the tranches which have an exercise price lower than the current share price of $20.00. ($7.5 million + $12.5 million + $15.0 million)

c. 2.0 million. Under the TSM, it is assumed that the $35.0 million is used to repurchase shares that are currently trading at $20.00. Therefore, the number of shares repurchased is 2.0 million ($35.0 million / $20.00). To calculate net new shares, the shares repurchased are subtracted from the total number of in-the-money options/warrants. (3.75 million shares − 1.75 million shares)

d. 125.0 million. Fully diluted shares are calculated as net new shares plus basic shares outstanding. (123.0 million shares + 2.0 million shares)

2) Calculation of equity value and enterprise value

($ in millions, except per share data; shares in millions)

Calculation of Equity and Enterprise Value	
Offer Price per Share	
Cash Offer Price per Share	$20.00
Stock Offer Price per Share	-
Exchange Ratio	-
Pearl Corp. Share Price	-
Offer Price per Share	$20.00
Fully Diluted Shares Outstanding	125.000
Implied Equity Value	**$2,500.0**
Implied Enterprise Value	
Plus: Total Debt	1,375.0
Plus: Preferred Stock	-
Plus: Noncontrolling Interest	-
Less: Cash and Cash Equivalents	(50.0)
Implied Enterprise Value	**$3,825.0**

= Equity Value + Total Debt - Cash
= $2,500.0 million + $1,375.0 million - $50.0 million

= Offer Price per Price x Fully Diluted Shares Outstanding
= $20.00 x 125.0 million

a. $2,500.0 million. Equity value is calculated by multiplying fully diluted shares outstanding by the offer price per share price. (125.0 million shares × $20.00)

b. $3,825.0 million. Enterprise value is calculated as equity value plus total debt minus cash and cash equivalents. ($2,500.0 million + $1,375.0 million – $50.0 million)

3) Adjusting for one-time and non-recurring items

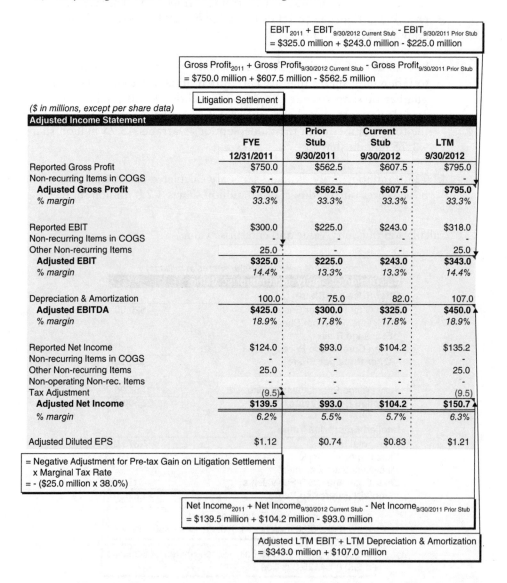

a. $795.0 million. LTM gross profit is calculated by taking the full prior fiscal year's gross profit, adding the YTD gross profit for the current year period ("current stub"), and then subtracting the YTD gross profit from the prior year ("prior stub"). ($750.0 million + $607.5 million – $562.5 million). In this case, no one-time adjustments are made as the $25.0 million litigation settlement is not included in COGS.

b. $343.0 million. To calculate adjusted LTM EBIT, first add back the $25.0 million litigation settlement for the fiscal year 2011 period. Next, the LTM statistic is calculated in the same manner as shown in 3(a). ($325.0 million + $243.0 million − $225.0 million)

c. $450.0 million. To calculate adjusted LTM EBITDA add LTM deprecation and amortization to LTM EBIT. ($343.0 million + $107.0 million)

d. $150.7 million. To calculate adjusted LTM net income, first add back the full litigation settlement charge to net income. Then, to make the tax adjustment, multiply the full add back amount by Rosenbaum's marginal tax rate. Next, the LTM statistic is calculated in the same manner as shown in 3(a). ($139.5 million + $104.2 million − $93.0 million)

4) Transaction multiples

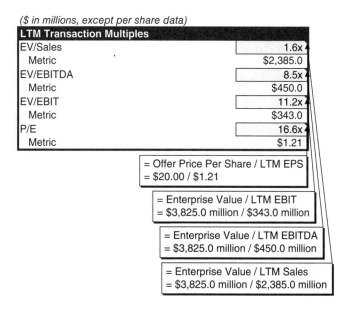

($ in millions, except per share data)

LTM Transaction Multiples	
EV/Sales	1.6x
Metric	$2,385.0
EV/EBITDA	8.5x
Metric	$450.0
EV/EBIT	11.2x
Metric	$343.0
P/E	16.6x
Metric	$1.21

= Offer Price Per Share / LTM EPS
= $20.00 / $1.21

= Enterprise Value / LTM EBIT
= $3,825.0 million / $343.0 million

= Enterprise Value / LTM EBITDA
= $3,825.0 million / $450.0 million

= Enterprise Value / LTM Sales
= $3,825.0 million / $2,385.0 million

a. 1.6x. Enterprise value-to-sales is calculated as enterprise value divided by LTM sales. ($3,825.0 million / $2,385.0 million)

b. 8.5x. Enterprise value-to-EBITDA is calculated as enterprise value divided by LTM EBITDA. ($3,825.0 million / $450.0 million)

c. 11.2x. Enterprise value-to-EBIT is calculated as enterprise value divided by LTM EBIT. ($3,825.0 million / $343.0 million)

d. 16.6x. Price-to-EPS is calculated as the offer price per share divided by LTM EPS. ($20.00 / $1.21)

5) Premiums paid

Premiums Paid		
Transaction Announcement		**Premium**
1 Day Prior	$17.39	15.0%
Unaffected Share Price		
1 Day Prior	$14.81	35.0%
7 Days Prior	15.04	33.0%
30 Days Prior	14.60	37.0%

= Offer Price per Price / Share Price One Day Prior to Unaffected - 1
= $20.00 / $14.60 - 1

= Offer Price per Price / Share Price 7 Days Prior to Unaffected - 1
= $20.00 / $15.04 - 1

= Offer Price per Price / Share Price 30 Days Prior to Unaffected - 1
= $20.00 / $14.81 - 1

= Offer Price per Price / Share Price One Day Prior to Announcement - 1
= $20.00 / $17.39 - 1

a. 15.0%. Premium paid one day prior to the transaction announcement is calculated as the offer price per share divided by the share price one day prior to announcement of the deal. ($20.00 / $17.39 − 1)

b. 35.0%. ($20.00 / $14.81 − 1)

c. 33.0%. ($20.00 / $15.04 − 1)

d. 37.0%. ($20.00 / $14.60 − 1)

6) Equity value and enterprise value calculations for precedent transactions

($ in millions)

Equity Value and Enterprise Value			
Acquirer	**Target**	**Equity Value**	**Enterprise Value**
Pearl Corp.	Rosenbaum Industries	$2,500.0	$3,825.0
Goodson Corp.	Schneider & Co.	5,048.8	6,173.8
Domanski Capital	Ackerman Industries	8,845.0	9,995.0

= Offer Price per Share x Fully Diluted Shares
= $37.25 x 135.5 million

= Equity Value + Total Debt - Total Cash
= $8,845.0 million + $1,250.0 million - $100.0 million

a. $5,048.8 million. Equity value is calculated as the offer price per share multiplied by fully diluted shares outstanding. ($37.25 × 135.5 million shares)

b. $9,995.0 million. Enterprise value is calculated as equity value plus total debt less total cash. ($8,845.0 million + $1,250.0 million – $100.0 million)

7) Precedent transaction multiples

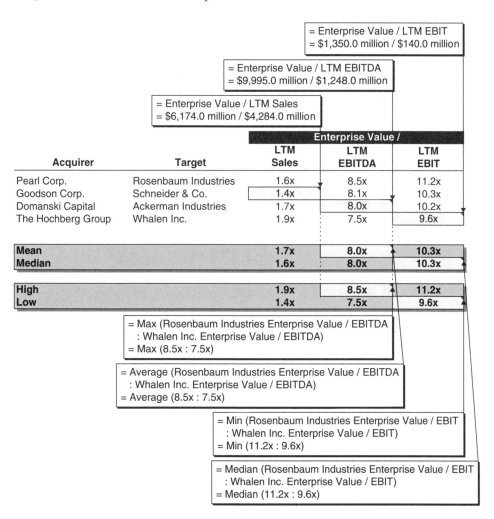

a. 1.4x. Enterprise value-to-sales is calculated as enterprise value divided by sales. ($6,174.0 million / $4,284.0 million)

b. 8.0x. ($9,995.0 million / $1,248.0 million)

c. 9.6x. ($1,350.0 million / $140.0 million)

d. 8.0x. The mean enterprise value-to-EBITDA multiple for the precedent transactions is calculated by taking the average of the enterprise value/EBITDA multiples for the precedent transactions

e. 10.3x. The median enterprise value-to-EBIT multiple for the precedent transactions is calculated by taking the average of the two middle numbers of the group as there are four transactions

f. 8.5x. The highest enterprise value-to-EBITDA multiple for the precedent transactions is the maximum enterprise value/EBITDA multiple for the precedent transactions

g. 9.6x. The lowest enterprise value-to-EBIT multiple for the precedent transactions is the minimum enterprise value/EBIT multiple for the precedent transactions

8) C. With the exception of credit reports, all of the other choices are common sources for creating an initial list of comparable acquisitions. Other resources include equity & fixed income research reports and merger proxies.

9) D. All of the questions are relevant to gain a better understanding of an M&A transaction.

10) D. All of the choices are reasons strategic buyers can often pay more for a target than financial sponsors under normal market conditions.

11) A. Enterprise value-to-LTM EBITDA and offer price-to-LTM diluted EPS are the most generic and widely-used multiples in precedent transactions analysis.

12) D. Speed of execution, certainty of completion, regulatory approvals, and other structural considerations are sometimes equally as important to a seller as the purchase price.

13) D. The proxy statement contains a summary of the background and terms of the transaction, a description of the financial analysis underlying the fairness opinion(s) of the financial advisor(s), a copy of the definitive purchase/sale agreement ("definitive agreement"), and summary and pro forma financial data (if applicable, depending on the form of consideration). The target's customer list is not contained in a proxy statement.

14) C. DEFM14A is a definitive proxy statement relating to an M&A transaction. The proxy statement contains the target's most recent basic share count, a detailed background of the merger, discussion of the premium paid, and an excerpt from the fairness opinion, among other items.

15) D. In an LBO of a public company where an "affiliate" (such as a senior company executive or significant shareholder) is part of the buyout group, the SEC requires broader disclosure of information used in the decision-making process on a Schedule 13E-3.

16) B. In a tender offer, an acquirer mails an Offer to Purchase to the target's shareholders and files a Schedule TO. The target must then file a Schedule 14D-9 within ten business days of the announcement of the tender. The Schedule 14D-9 contains a recommendation from the target's board of directors to the target's shareholders on how to respond to the tender offer.

17) D. A private acquirer does not need to file an 8-K as it is not subject to SEC disclosure requirements. For a public acquirer, an acquisition is required to be reported in an 8-K if the assets, income, or value of the target comprise 10% or greater of the acquirer's.

18) B. Purchase consideration refers to the mix of cash, stock, and/or other securities that the acquirer offers to the target's shareholders. In some cases, the form of consideration can affect the target shareholders' perception of the value embedded in the offer. For example, some shareholders may prefer cash over stock as payment due to its guaranteed value.

19) A. Scarcity value refers to a rare or highly desired asset that may be critical to an acquirer's strategic plan.

20) C. A fixed exchange ratio is most common. A fixed exchange ratio defines the number of shares of the acquirer's stock to be exchanged for each share of the target's stock. In a floating exchange ratio, the number of acquirer shares exchanged for target shares fluctuates so as to ensure a fixed value for the target's shareholders.

21) A. Synergies refer to the expected cost savings, growth opportunities, and other financial benefits that occur as a result of the combination of two businesses. On the cost side, traditional synergies include headcount reduction,

consolidation of overlapping facilities, and the ability to buy key inputs at lower prices due to increased purchasing power.

22) C. Financial characteristics, timing, and size of the companies should all be taken into consideration when selecting precedent transactions. Other factors include consideration paid and market conditions.

23) A. A fixed exchange ratio defines the number of shares of the acquirer's stock to be exchanged for each share of the target's stock. The fixed exchange ratio of 0.25 is determined by dividing 0.5 by 2.

24) A. See calculation below:

($ in millions, except per share data; shares in millions)

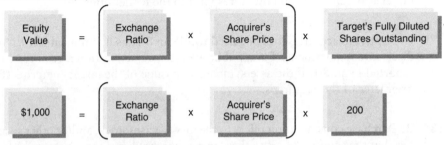

25) In a fixed exchange ratio structure, the offer price per share (value to target) moves in line with the underlying share price of the acquirer. The amount of the acquirer's shares received, however, is constant.

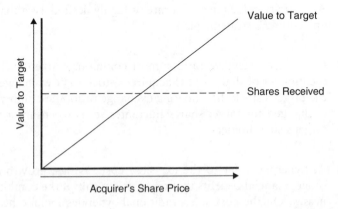

26) In a floating exchange ratio structure, as opposed to a fixed exchange ratio, the dollar offer price per share (value to target) is set and the number of shares exchanged fluctuates in accordance with the movement of the acquirer's share price.

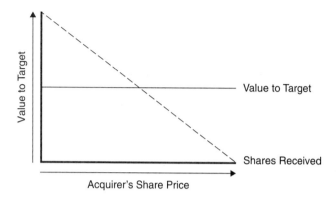

27) B. In a floating exchange ratio structure, the offer price per share is set while the number of shares exchanged fluctuates. Therefore, this structure presents target shareholders with greater certainty in terms of value received because the acquirer assumes the full risk of a decline in its share price.

28) A. A floating exchange ratio is generally used when the acquirer is significantly larger than the target. It is justified in these cases on the basis that while a significant decline in the target's business does not materially impact the value of the acquirer, the reciprocal is not true.

29) C. See calculation below:

($ in millions, except per share data; shares in millions)

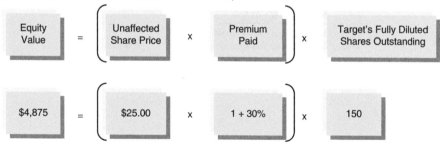

30) D. See calculation below:

($ in millions, except per share data; shares in millions)

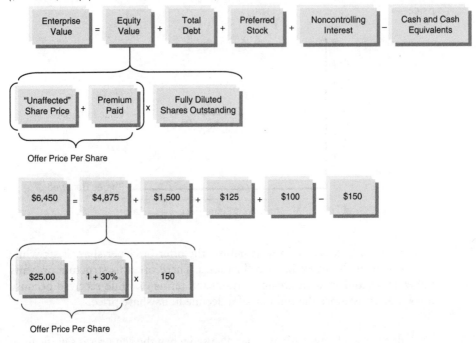

31) D. See calculation below:

32) A. See calculation below:

33) B. Precedent transactions, by definition, have occurred in the past and, therefore, may not be truly reflective of prevailing market conditions (e.g., the LBO boom in the mid-2000s vs. the ensuing credit crunch).

34) B. Synergies refer to the expected cost savings, growth opportunities, and other financial benefits that occur as a result of the combination of two businesses. They can be broken down into revenue and cost synergies.

35) D. Relativity – multiples approach provides straightforward reference points across sectors and time periods.

36) D. All of the answer choices are useful strategies for locating comparable acquisitions. Others include equity and fixed income reports.

37) A. The exchange ratio is determined by dividing the offer price per share by the acquirer's share price. $15.00 / $30.00 = 0.50

38) C. The premium paid is calculated by dividing the offer price per share by the target's unaffected share price and then subtracting 1. ($15.00 / $12.00) – 1) = 20%

39) A. See calculation below:

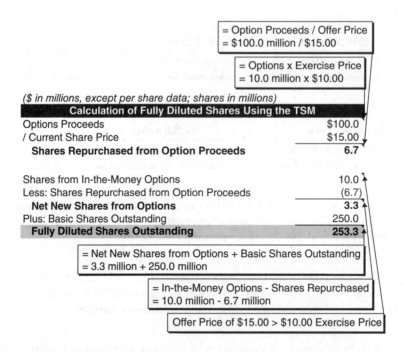

= Option Proceeds / Offer Price
= $100.0 million / $15.00

= Options x Exercise Price
= 10.0 million x $10.00

($ in millions, except per share data; shares in millions)

Calculation of Fully Diluted Shares Using the TSM

Options Proceeds	$100.0
/ Current Share Price	$15.00
Shares Repurchased from Option Proceeds	**6.7**
Shares from In-the-Money Options	10.0
Less: Shares Repurchased from Option Proceeds	(6.7)
Net New Shares from Options	**3.3**
Plus: Basic Shares Outstanding	250.0
Fully Diluted Shares Outstanding	**253.3**

= Net New Shares from Options + Basic Shares Outstanding
= 3.3 million + 250.0 million

= In-the-Money Options - Shares Repurchased
= 10.0 million - 6.7 million

Offer Price of $15.00 > $10.00 Exercise Price

40) A. See calculation below:

($ in millions, except per share data; shares in millions)

Calculation of Offer Value and Enterprise Value

Fully Diluted Shares Outstanding	253.3
x Offer Price Per Share	$15.00
Offer Value	**$3,800.0**
Plus: Net Debt	1,000.0
Enterprise Value	**$4,800.0**

41) D. Enterprise value-to-EBITDA is calculated by dividing enterprise value by LTM EBITDA. ($4,800 million / $650 million)

42) A. Enterprise value-to-sales is calculated by dividing enterprise value by LTM sales. ($4,800 million / $4,500 million)

43) Precedent transactions analysis, like comparable companies analysis, employs a multiples-based approach to derive an implied valuation range for a given company, division, business, or collection of assets ("target"). It is premised on multiples paid for comparable companies in prior M&A transactions.

44) Whether acquired companies have similar business and financial characteristics as the company being valued. The banker must also examine market conditions and dynamics, and, potentially, deal structure.

45) Traditionally, strategic buyers have been able to pay higher purchase prices than financial sponsors due to their potential ability to realize synergies from the target, among other factors, including lower cost of capital and return thresholds, as well as a longer investment time horizon.

46) A strategic buyer may stretch to pay a higher price for an asset if there are substantial synergies to be realized or the asset is critical to its strategic plan. A corporation in need of cash that is selling a non-core business, for example, may prioritize speed of execution, certainty of completion, and other structural considerations, which may result in a lower valuation than a pure value maximization strategy. A quality asset sold to a sponsor in a robust auction during the credit boom might have resulted in a higher valuation.

47) Hostile transactions may increase cost to the acquirer due to the need to tender shares at a premium directly from shareholders. They may also create a bidding war between the hostile party and another buyer.

48) It is based the "unaffected" share price, typically the share price at various intervals prior to transaction announcement (e.g., 1, 7, and 30 days prior).

49) This would happen in the event of the announcement of a company's decision to pursue strategic alternatives, leaks to the public, or rumors prior to transaction announcement.

50) Synergies are most common when a strategic buyer is purchasing a target company that operates a similar or related business. The acquirer and target often have overlap in facilities/people that can be eliminated.

51)   In order to receive credit from investors for potential value creation.

52)   Premium paid refers to the incremental dollar amount per share that the acquirer offers relative to the target's unaffected share price, expressed as a percentage. As such, it is only relevant for public target companies. In calculating the premium paid relative to a given date, it is important to use the target's unaffected share price so as to isolate the true effect of the purchase offer.

53)   The full projections that an acquirer uses to frame its purchase price decision are generally not public and subject to a confidentiality agreement. Therefore, the banker must use LTM financial data as it can be calculated from publicly available data.

54)   The higher end, typically above comparable companies and LBO analysis.

55)   First, buyers generally pay a "control premium" when purchasing another company. In return for this premium, the acquirer receives the right to control decisions regarding the target's business and its underlying cash flows. Second, strategic buyers often have the opportunity to realize synergies, which supports the ability to pay higher purchase prices.

56)   This could happen if the particular sector is "in play" or has high growth expectations potentially due to the point in the cycle.

57)   Benefits of using precedent transactions:

  ▪ *Market-based* – analysis is based on actual acquisition multiples and premiums paid for similar companies

  ▪ *Current* – recent transactions tend to reflect prevailing M&A, capital markets, and general economic conditions

  ▪ *Relativity* – multiples approach provides straightforward reference points across sectors and time periods

  ▪ *Simplicity* – key multiples for a few selected transactions can anchor valuation

  ▪ *Objectivity* – precedent-based and, therefore, avoids making assumptions about a company's future performance

58) Considerations when using precedent transactions:

■ *Market-based* – multiples may be skewed depending on capital markets and/or economic environment at the time of the transaction

■ *Time lag* – precedent transactions, by definition, have occurred in the past and, therefore, may not be truly reflective of prevailing market conditions (e.g., the LBO boom in the mid-2000s vs. the ensuing credit crunch)

■ *Existence of comparable acquisitions* – in some cases it may be difficult to find a robust universe of precedent transactions

■ *Availability of information* – information may be insufficient to determine transaction multiples for many comparable acquisitions

■ *Acquirer's basis for valuation* – multiple paid by the buyer may be based on expectations governing the target's future financial performance (which is typically not publicly disclosed) rather than on reported LTM financial information

CHAPTER 3

Discounted Cash Flow Analysis

1) Using the information and assumptions below, complete ValueCo's projected income statement through EBITDA

Assumptions	
Sales	7.5% growth in 2013, 6.0% growth in 2014, then decreasing 1% per year thereafter
COGS	60.0% of sales, hold constant throughout projection period
SG&A	19.0% of sales, hold constant throughout projection period

ValueCo Corporation
($ in millions, fiscal year ending December 31)

	Historical Period			
	2009	**2010**	**2011**	**2012**
Sales	**$2,600.0**	**$2,900.0**	**$3,200.0**	**$3,450.0**
% growth	*NA*	*11.5%*	*10.3%*	*7.8%*
Cost of Goods Sold	1,612.0	1,769.0	1,920.0	2,070.0
Gross Profit	**$988.0**	**$1,131.0**	**$1,280.0**	**$1,380.0**
% margin	*38.0%*	*39.0%*	*40.0%*	*40.0%*
Selling, General & Administrative	496.6	551.0	608.0	655.0
EBITDA	**$491.4**	**$580.0**	**$672.0**	**$725.0**
% margin	*18.9%*	*20.0%*	*21.0%*	*21.0%*

	Projection Period				
	2013	**2014**	**2015**	**2016**	**2017**
Sales	A)				
% growth					
COGS		B)			
Gross Profit			C)		
% margin					
SG&A				D)	
EBITDA					E)

   a. Calculate ValueCo's 2013 sales

_____

   b. Calculate 2014 COGS

_____

   c. Calculate 2015 gross profit

---

   d. Calculate 2016 SG&A

---

   e. Calculate 2017 EBITDA

---

2) Using the prior answers and information, as well as the assumptions below, complete ValueCo's projected income statement through EBIAT

Assumptions

D&A	6.0% of sales, hold constant throughout projection period
Tax Rate	38.0%, hold constant throughout projection period

ValueCo Corporation
($ in millions, fiscal year ending December 31)

	Historical Period			
	2009	2010	2011	2012
EBITDA	$491.4	$580.0	$672.0	$725.0
Depreciation & Amortization	155.0	165.0	193.0	207.0
EBIT	$336.4	$415.0	$479.0	$518.0
% margin	*12.9%*	*14.3%*	*15.0%*	*15.0%*
Taxes	127.8	157.7	182.0	196.8
EBIAT	$208.6	$257.3	$297.0	$321.2

	Projection Period				
	2013	2014	2015	2016	2017
EBITDA					
D&A	A)				
EBIT		B)			
% margin					
Taxes			C)		
EBIAT				D)	

a. Calculate ValueCo's 2013 D&A

_____

b. Calculate 2014 EBIT

_____

c. Calculate 2015 taxes

_____

d. Calculate 2016 EBIAT

_____

3) Using the information below, calculate ValueCo's 2011 working capital ratios

ValueCo Corporation
Working Capital Projections
($ in millions, fiscal year ending December 31)

| | Historical Period | | | |
	2009	2010	2011	2012
Sales	$2,600.0	$2,900.0	$3,200.0	$3,450.0
Cost of Goods Sold	1,612.0	1,769.0	1,920.0	2,070.0
Current Assets				
Accounts Receivable	317.0	365.5	417.4	450.0
Inventories	441.6	496.8	556.5	600.0
Prepaid Expenses and Other	117.0	142.1	162.3	175.0
Total Current Assets	**$875.6**	**$1,004.4**	**$1,136.2**	**$1,225.0**
Current Liabilities				
Accounts Payable	189.9	189.0	199.4	215.0
Accrued Liabilities	221.0	237.8	255.1	275.0
Other Current Liabilities	75.4	84.1	92.8	100.0
Total Current Liabilities	**$486.3**	**$510.9**	**$547.2**	**$590.0**
Net Working Capital	**$389.4**	**$493.5**	**$589.0**	**$635.0**
% sales	*15.0%*	*17.0%*	*18.4%*	*18.4%*
(Increase)/Decrease in NWC		($104.1)	($95.5)	($46.0)

Assumptions

Current Assets			
Days Sales Outstanding	44.5	46.0	A)
Days Inventory Held	100.0	102.5	B)
Prepaids and Other CA (% of sales)	4.5%	4.9%	C)

Current Liabilities			
Days Payable Outstanding	43.0	39.0	D)
Accrued Liabilities (% of sales)	8.5%	8.2%	E)
Other Current Liabilities (% of sales)	2.9%	2.9%	F)

a. Calculate ValueCo's 2011 days sales outstanding (DSO)

b. Calculate 2011 days inventory held (DIH)

c. Calculate 2011 prepaid and other current assets as a percentage of sales

   d. Calculate 2011 days payable outstanding (DPO)

   e. Calculate 2011 accrued liabilities as a percentage of sales

   f. Calculate 2011 other current liabilities as a percentage of sales

4) Using the prior answers and information, as well as the assumptions below, complete ValueCo's working capital projections. Hold 2011/2012 working capital ratios constant

ValueCo Corporation
Working Capital Projections
($ in millions, fiscal year ending December 31)

	Projection Period				
	2013	2014	2015	2016	2017
Sales					
Cost of Goods Sold					
Current Assets					
Accounts Receivable	A)				
Inventories		B)			
Prepaid Expenses and Other			C)		
Total Current Assets				D)	
Current Liabilities					
Accounts Payable	E)				
Accrued Liabilities		F)			
Other Current Liabilities			G)		
Total Current Liabilities				H)	
Net Working Capital					I)
(Inc.)/Dec. in NWC					J)

   a. Calculate ValueCo's 2013 accounts receivable

b. Calculate 2014 inventories

_____

c. Calculate 2015 prepaid expenses and other current liabilities

_____

d. Calculate 2016 total current assets

_____

e. Calculate 2013 accounts payable

_____

f. Calculate 2014 accrued liabilities

_____

g. Calculate 2015 other current liabilities

_____

h. Calculate 2016 total current liabilities

_____

i. Calculate 2017 net working capital

_____

j. Calculate 2017 (increase)/decrease in net working capital

_____

5) Using the prior answers and information, as well as the assumptions below, complete ValueCo's projected free cash flow

Assumptions

Capital Expenditures   4.5% of sales, hold constant throughout projection period

ValueCo Corporation

($ in millions, fiscal year ending December 31)

	Historical Period			
	2009	2010	2011	2012
EBIAT	$208.6	$257.3	$297.0	$321.2
Plus: D&A	155.0	165.0	193.0	207.0
Less: Capex	(114.4)	(116.0)	(144.0)	(155.3)
Less: Inc./(Dec.) in NWC				
Unlevered FCF				

	Projection Period				
	2013	2014	2015	2016	2017
EBIAT					
Plus: D&A					
Less: Capex	A)				
Less: Inc./(Dec.) in NWC					
Unlevered FCF		B)			

a. Calculate ValueCo's 2013 capital expenditures

b. Calculate 2014 free cash flow

6) Using the assumptions for ValueCo below, complete the following questions regarding the weighted average cost of capital

Assumptions	
Debt-to-Total Capitalization	30.0%
Cost of Debt	6.0%
Tax Rate	38.0%
Risk-free Rate	3.0%
Market Risk Premium	6.6%
Size Premium	1.1%

a. Calculate ValueCo's equity-to-total capitalization

b. Calculate ValueCo's debt-to-equity ratio

c. Calculate ValueCo's after-tax cost of debt

($ in millions)

Comparable Companies Unlevered Beta						
Company	Predicted Levered Beta	Market Value of Debt	Market Value of Equity	Debt/ Equity	Marginal Tax Rate	Unlevered Beta
BuyerCo	1.24	$2,200.0	$9,800.0 D)		38.0%	
Sherman Co.	1.35	3,150.0	5,600.0		38.0% E)	
Gasparro Corp.	1.25	1,850.0	5,000.0		38.0%	
Goodson Corp	1.45	2,250.0	4,160.0		38.0%	
S. Momper & Co.	1.14	1,000.0	2,240.0		38.0%	
Mean	1.29			F)		G)
Median	1.25			44.6%		1.02

d. Calculate BuyerCo's debt-to-equity ratio

e. Calculate Sherman Co.'s unlevered beta

f. Calculate the mean debt-to-equity ratio for the comparable companies

_____

g. Calculate the mean unlevered beta for the comparable companies

_____

h. Using the mean unlevered beta for the comparable companies, determine ValueCo's relevered beta

ValueCo Relevered Beta				
	Mean Unlevered Beta	Target Debt/ Equity	Target Marginal Tax Rate	Relevered Beta
Relevered Beta				

_____

i. Calculate ValueCo's cost-of-equity

Cost of Equity	
Risk-free Rate	
Market Risk Premium	
Levered Beta	
Size Premium	
Cost of Equity	

_____

j. Calculate ValueCo's WACC

WACC Calculation

Target Capital Structure
Debt-to-Total Capitalization
Equity-to-Total Capitalization

Cost of Debt
Cost-of-Debt
Tax Rate
   After-tax Cost of Debt

Cost of Equity
Risk-free Rate
Market Risk Premium
Levered Beta
Size Premium
   Cost of Equity

   WACC

7) Using the prior answers and information as well as the assumptions below, complete the questions regarding ValueCo's terminal value

a. Using an exit multiple of 7.5x, calculate the terminal value using the exit multiple method

($ in millions)

Calculation of Terminal Value using EMM	
Terminal Year EBITDA (2017E)	
Exit Multiple	7.5x
Terminal Value	

b. Assuming a mid-year convention and using the terminal value found in 7(a), calculate the implied perpetuity growth rate

($ in millions)

Implied Perpetuity Growth Rate	
Terminal Year Free Cash Flow (2017E)	
Discount Rate	
Terminal Value	
Implied Perpetuity Growth Rate	

c. Using a 3% perpetuity growth rate, calculate the terminal value using the perpetuity growth method

($ in millions)

Calculation of Terminal Value using PGM	
Terminal Year Free Cash Flow (2017E)	
WACC	
Perpetuity Growth Rate	3.0%
Terminal Value	

d. Using the terminal value found in 7(c), calculate the implied exit multiple

($ in millions)

Implied Exit Multiple	
Terminal Value	
Terminal Year EBITDA (2017E)	
WACC	
Implied Exit Multiple	

8) Using the prior answers and information, complete the questions below regarding present value, assuming a mid-year convention

($ in millions)

Present Value Calculation

		Projection Period			
	2013	**2014**	**2015**	**2016**	**2017**
Unlevered Free Cash Flow					
WACC					
Discount Period	A)				
Discount Factor	0.95	B)		0.79	0.72	0.65
Present Value of Free Cash Flow			C)		

Terminal Value

Terminal Year EBITDA (2017E)					
Exit Multiple					7.5x
Terminal Value					
Discount Factor					D)
Present Value of Terminal Value					E)

a. Determine ValueCo's 2013 discount period

b. Calculate the 2014 discount factor

c. Calculate the 2015 present value of free cash flow

d. Assuming the exit multiple method is used, determine the appropriate terminal value discount factor

_____

e. Calculate the present value of the terminal value

_____

9) Using the prior answers and information, complete the questions below regarding ValueCo's enterprise value

($ in millions)

Enterprise Value	
Cumulative Present Value of FCF	**A)**
Terminal Value	
Terminal Year EBITDA (2017E)	
Exit Multiple	
Terminal Value	
Discount Factor	
Present Value of Terminal Value	
% of Enterprise Value	**C)**
Enterprise Value	**B)**

a. Calculate the cumulative present value of FCF for 2013E – 2017E

_____

b. Calculate enterprise value

_____

c. Determine the percentage of enterprise value represented by the terminal value

_____

10) Using the prior answers and information, complete the questions below regarding ValueCo's equity value and implied share price

($ in millions)

Assumptions	
Total Debt	$1,500.0
Cash and Cash Equivalents	250.0

Implied Equity Value and Share Price	
Enterprise Value	
Less: Total Debt	
Less: Preferred Stock	
Less: Noncontrolling Interest	
Plus: Cash and Cash Equivalents	
Implied Equity Value	

a. Calculate ValueCo's implied equity value

Use the table below to answer 10(b) and 10(c). Note: use the Iteration Function in Microsoft Excel

Options/Warrants		
Tranche	Number of Shares	Exercise Price
Tranche 1	2.250	$25.00
Tranche 2	1.000	30.00
Tranche 3	0.750	45.00
Tranche 4	0.500	57.50
Tranche 5	0.250	75.00

b. Assuming 80 million basic shares outstanding, calculate fully diluted shares outstanding

c. Calculate ValueCo's implied share price

11) Which of the following is the correct order of the steps to complete a DCF analysis?

    I. Determine Terminal Value
    II. Study the Target and Determine Key Performance Drivers
    III. Calculate Present Value and Determine Valuation
    IV. Project Free Cash Flow
    V. Calculate Weighted Average Cost of Capital

    A. II, V, IV, III, and I
    B. II, IV, V, I, and III
    C. III, IV, V, I, and II
    D. III, IV, V, II, and I

12) Which of the following is a current asset?

    A. Goodwill
    B. Property, plant and equipment
    C. Accrued liabilities
    D. Prepaid expenses

13) Which of the following is a long-term asset?

    A. Goodwill
    B. Prepaid expenses
    C. Accounts payable
    D. Accounts receivable

14) Calculate FCF using the information below

($ in millions)	
Assumptions	
EBIT	$300.0
Depreciation & Amortization	50.0
Capital Expenditures	25.0
Inc./(Dec.) in Net Working Capital	10.0
Tax Rate	38.0%

    A. $151.0 million
    B. $189.0 million
    C. $201.0 million
    D. $211.0 million

15) Calculate FCF using the information below

($ in millions)	
Assumptions	
Sales	$1,000.0
EBITDA margin	15.0%
Depreciation & Amortization % of sales	3.0%
Capital Expenditures % of sales	2.5%
Inc./(Dec.) in Net Working Capital	15.0
Tax Rate	38.0%

   A. $64.4 million
   B. $79.4 million
   C. $89.1 million
   D. $102.0 million

16) Which of the following are relevant for creating assumptions when projecting FCF in a DCF?

   I. Historical interest expense
   II. Historical growth rates
   III. Classes of debt securities
   VI. Historical EBIT margins

   A. I and II
   B. I and III
   C. II and IV
   D. I, II, III, and IV

17) How long is the typical DCF projection period?

   A. 1 year
   B. 3 years
   C. 5 years
   D. 30 years

18) Which of the following factors help determine the length of the projection period?

    I. Sector
    II. Predictability of FCF
   III. Business model
   IV. Maturity of business

    A. I and II
    B. II and III
    C. II and IV
    D. I, II, III, and IV

19) For which type of company might a 15 to 20 year projection period be appropriate?

    A. Company with long-term contracted revenue streams
    B. Company that sells its product and services in many countries
    C. Company that offers several products and services
    D. Company with a low cost of capital

20) For which of the following companies would the DCF projection period most likely be longer than five years?

    A. Utility
    B. Capital goods
    C. Retailer
    D. Automotive

21) Which of the following are key variables commonly sensitized in the DCF?

    I. WACC
    II. Exit multiple
   III. IRR
   IV. EBIT margins

    A. I and III
    B. II and III
    C. I, II, and IV
    D. I, III, and IV

22) Which of the following types of companies would be expected to have high capital expenditures?

    I. Mining company
    II. Heavy equipment manufacturer
    III. Mature distributor
    IV. Oil and gas company

    A. I, II, and III
    B. I, II, and IV
    C. I, III, and IV
    D. I, II, III, and IV

23) Which of the following is NOT a key driver of a company's projected FCF?

    A. Capital expenditures
    B. Sales growth
    C. EBIT margins
    D. Discount rate

24) Beta is a measure of the covariance between _____ and _____.

    A. Rate of return on a company's stock; overall market return
    B. Rate of return on a company's stock; market return for the company's sector
    C. Rate of return on a company's bonds; overall market return
    D. Rate of return on a company's stock; market return for its bonds

25) The CAPM is based on the premise that equity investors need to be compensated for their assumption of

    A. Systematic risk
    B. Unsystematic risk
    C. Default risk
    D. Risk of financial distress

26) A stock with a beta greater than 1.0 has

    A. Lower systematic risk than the market
    B. Higher systematic risk than the market
    C. Lower unsystematic risk than the market
    D. Higher unsystematic risk than the market

27) A company with no debt in its capital structure would have a WACC equal to its

    A. Cost of debt
    B. Risk-free rate
    C. Tax-effected cost of equity
    D. Cost of equity

28) Which of the following are common characteristics of BOTH depreciation and amortization?

    I. Non-cash expense
    II. Reduce reported earnings
    III. Reduce intangible assets
    IV. Not included on the cash flow statement

    A. I and II
    B. II and III
    C. I, II, and IV
    D. II, III, and IV

29) Capex and depreciation share all of the following characteristics EXCEPT

    A. Used in the calculation of FCF
    B. Represent actual cash outflows
    C. Found on the cash flow statement
    D. Included in the calculation of PP&E

30) Calculate the (increase) / decrease in net working capital from 2012 to 2013 based on the following assumptions

($ in millions)

Assumptions	2012	2013
Accounts Receivable	$325.0	$350.0
Inventories	200.0	210.0
Prepaid Expenses and Other	35.0	45.0
Accounts Payable	300.0	315.0
Accrued Liabilities	150.0	160.0
Other Current Liabilities	60.0	65.0

    A. $10.0 million
    B. ($10.0) million
    C. $15.0 million
    D. ($15.0) million

31) An increase in inventory is

    A. A use of cash
    B. A source of cash
    C. No change in cash
    D. A decrease in PP&E

32) An increase in accounts payable is

    A. A use of cash
    B. A source of cash
    C. No change in cash
    D. An increase in PP&E

33) What does days sales outstanding measure?

    A. Number of days it takes to collect payment after the sale of a product or service
    B. Number of days a customer is overdue on their payment
    C. Number of days a customer has remaining to pay their balance
    D. Number of days it takes to make payment on outstanding purchases of goods and services

34) Calculate DSO assuming a company has $3.5 billion in revenue and $300 million in accounts receivable

    A. 29 days
    B. 30 days
    C. 31 days
    D. 43 days

35) What does days inventory held measure?

    A. Number of days before a company's inventory becomes obsolete
    B. Number of days it takes a company to receive new inventory
    C. Number of days it takes a company to pay for its inventory
    D. Number of days it takes a company to sell its inventory

36) What does inventory turns measure?

    A. Number of times a company turns over its inventory per month
    B. Number of times a company turns over its inventory per quarter
    C. Number of times a company turns over its inventory per year
    D. Number of times a company turns over its inventory per season

37) Calculate DIH assuming a company has $3.5 billion in revenue, $2.4 billion in COGs, and $525 million in inventory

    A. 70 days
    B. 75 days
    C. 80 days
    D. 85 days

38) Calculate inventory turns using the information found in the prior question

    A. 4.6x
    B. 4.9x
    C. 5.1x
    D. 6.1x

39) What does days payable outstanding measure?

    A. Number of days a customer is given to make payment
    B. Number of days it takes a company to collect payment after sale of a product or service
    C. Number of days it takes a company to make payment on outstanding fixed expenses
    D. Number of days it takes a company to make payment on outstanding purchases of goods and services

40) Calculate DPO assuming a company has $4.3 billion in revenue, $3.3 billion in COGs, and $250 million in accounts payable

    A. 28 days
    B. 30 days
    C. 32 days
    D. 33 days

41) What method is used to calculate cost of equity?

    A. WACC
    B. CAPM
    C. NWC
    D. YTW

42) Which of the following is an acceptable proxy for the risk-free rate in the CAPM?

    A. The company's after-tax cost of debt
    B. The Fed Funds Rate
    C. The interpolated yield on a 20-year Treasury bond
    D. The London Interbank Offered Rate

43) Which of the following is the most appropriate market risk premium to use in the calculation of cost of equity?

    A. 0%-1%
    B. 2%-3%
    C. 6%-7%
    D. 10%+

44) Calculate cost of equity using the information below

Assumptions	
Levered Beta	1.25
Risk-free Rate	3.0%
Market Risk Premium	6.6%
Cost of Debt	9.0%

    A. 11.3%
    B. 12.0%
    C. 13.1%
    D. 14.4%

45) Which of the following sectors should have the lowest beta?

    A. Social media
    B. Utility
    C. Homebuilder
    D. Chemicals

46) Calculate unlevered beta using the information below

Assumptions	
Levered Beta	1.25
Debt / Equity Ratio	40.0%
Marginal Tax Rate	38.0%

A. 0.83
B. 1.00
C. 1.12
D. 1.35

47) Calculate levered beta using the information below

Assumptions	
Unlevered Beta	1.00
Debt / Equity Ratio	45.0%
Marginal Tax Rate	38.0%

A. 1.01
B. 1.25
C. 1.28
D. 1.42

48) Which methodology is used to capture the value of a company beyond its projection period?

A. Long-term value
B. Long-term adjusted value
C. Terminal value
D. Projected value

49) Calculate terminal value using the assumptions below

($ in millions)

Assumptions	
Year 5 FCF	$250.0
Growth Rate	3.0%
WACC	12.0%

A. $2,800.2 million
B. $2,861.1 million
C. $3,111.5 million
D. $3,215.2 million

50) How does using a mid-year convention affect valuation in a DCF?

    A. Higher value than year-end discounting
    B. Lower value than year-end discounting
    C. Same value as year-end discounting
    D. Not applicable

51) A company is expected to generate $500 million of free cash flow over the next year and has a weighted average cost of capital of 12%. What is the present value of the company's free cash flow using mid-year discounting?

    A. $529.2 million
    B. $421.8 million
    C. $446.4 million
    D. $472.5 million

52) How does using a mid-year convention affect the PGM and EMM?

    A. Mid-year convention is used in PGM; year-end is used in EMM
    B. Mid-year convention is used in EMM; year-end is used in PGM
    C. Mid-year convention is used in both PGM and EMM
    D. Mid-year convention is not used in PGM or EMM

53) Using a mid-year convention and the assumptions below, calculate enterprise value

($ in millions)			
Assumptions			
FCF 2013E	$100.0	Terminal Multiple	7.5x
FCF 2014E	110.0	WACC	10.0%
FCF 2015E	120.0		
FCF 2016E	125.0		
FCF 2017E	130.0		
EBITDA 2017E	250.0		

    A. $1,710 million
    B. $1,725 million
    C. $1,624 million
    D. $1,986 million

54) Why might perpetuity growth method be used instead of exit multiple method?

    A. Absence of relevant comparables to determine an exit multiple
    B. Difficult to determine a long-term growth rate
    C. Current economic environment is volatile
    D. Target company is private

55) Which terminal value formula requires a steady state at the end of the projection period?

    A. PGM
    B. EMM
    C. Both
    D. Neither

56) Which method is preferred to determine cost of debt for the WACC calculation if the target company's debt is not traded?

    A. Historical average interest expense
    B. Spread between CAPM and risk-free rate
    C. Calculate by determining implied credit rating and yield, based on target capital structure
    D. None of the above

57) Which one of the following is considered a weakness of the DCF?

    A. Market independent
    B. Terminal value represents a large portion of the total value
    C. Can handle multiple financial performance scenarios
    D. Minimal reliance on comparable companies or transactions

58) Why may a banker choose to add a size premium to the CAPM formula?

    A. Empirical evidence suggesting that smaller companies are riskier and, therefore, should have a higher cost of equity
    B. Empirical evidence suggesting that larger companies are riskier and, therefore, should have a higher cost of equity.
    C. To compensate for the market risk premium, which can vary
    D. To compensate for the risk-free rate, which can vary

59) What are some of the challenges with projecting FCF for cyclical companies?

_____

_____

_____

_____

60) What are some of the considerations to take into account when projecting terminal year FCF for a cyclical company?

_____

_____

_____

_____

61) How is depreciation reflected on the a) income statement, b) cash flow statement, and c) balance sheet?

_____

_____

_____

_____

62) All else being equal, if WACC increases, does enterprise value increase or decrease? Why?

_____

_____

_____

_____

63) What would be the impact on valuation of using a 5.0% market risk premium versus an 8% market risk premium?

_____

_____

_____

_____

64) What are some of the benefits of using DCF analysis?

_____

_____

_____

_____

65) What are some of the considerations when using DCF analysis?

_____

_____

_____

_____

1) ValueCo's projected income statement through EBITDA

= Sales$_{2014E}$ x % of Sales
= $3,931.3 million x 60.0%

= Sales$_{2012}$ x (1 + Growth Rate)
= $3,450.0 million x (1 + 7.5%)

ValueCo Corporation
($ in millions, fiscal year ending December 31)

	Projection Period				
	2013	2014	2015	2016	2017
Sales	**$3,708.8**	**$3,931.3**	**$4,127.8**	**$4,293.0**	**$4,421.7**
% growth	7.5%	6.0%	5.0%	4.0%	3.0%
COGS	2,225.3	2,358.8	2,476.7	2,575.8	2,653.0
Gross Profit	**$1,483.5**	**$1,572.5**	**$1,651.1**	**$1,717.2**	**$1,768.7**
% margin	40.0%	40.0%	40.0%	40.0%	40.0%
SG&A	704.1	746.4	783.7	815.0	839.5
EBITDA	**$779.4**	**$826.1**	**$867.4**	**$902.1**	**$929.2**
% margin	21.0%	21.0%	21.0%	21.0%	21.0%

= Sales$_{2015E}$ - COGS$_{2015E}$
= $4,127.8 million - $2,476.7 million

= Sales$_{2016E}$ x % of Sales
= $4,293.0 million x 19.0%

= Gross Profit$_{2017E}$ - SG&A$_{2017E}$
= $1,768.7 million - $839.5 million

a. $3,708.8 million. 2013 sales is calculated as 2012 sales multiplied by one plus a 7.5% growth rate. ($3,450.0 million × (1 + 7.5%))

b. $2,358.8 million. 2014 cost of goods sold is calculated as 2014 sales multiplied by 60%. ($3,931.3 million × 60%)

c. $1,651.1 million. 2015 gross profit is calculated as 2015 sales less 2015 cost of goods sold. ($4,127.8 million - $2,476.7 million)

d. $815.0 million. 2016 selling, general & administrative is calculated as 2016 sales multiplied by 19%. ($4,293.0 × 19%)

e. $929.2 million. 2017 EBITDA is calculated as 2017 gross profit less 2017 selling, general & administrative expense. ($1,768.7 million - $839.5 million)

2) ValueCo's projected income statement through EBIAT

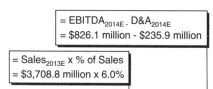

$$= \text{EBITDA}_{2014E} - \text{D\&A}_{2014E}$$
$$= \$826.1 \text{ million} - \$235.9 \text{ million}$$

$$= \text{Sales}_{2013E} \times \% \text{ of Sales}$$
$$= \$3,708.8 \text{ million} \times 6.0\%$$

ValueCo Corporation
($ in millions, fiscal year ending December 31)

	2013	Projection Period 2014	2015	2016	2017
EBITDA	$779.4	$826.1	$867.4	$902.1	$929.2
D&A	222.5	235.9	247.7	257.6	265.3
EBIT	$556.9	$590.3	$619.8	$644.6	$663.9
% margin	*15.0%*	*15.0%*	*15.0%*	*15.0%*	*15.0%*
Taxes	211.6	224.3	235.5	244.9	252.3
EBIAT	$345.2	$366.0	$384.3	$399.6	$411.6

$$= \text{EBIT}_{2015E} \times \text{Tax Rate}$$
$$= \$619.8 \text{ million} \times 38.0\%$$

$$= \text{EBITDA}_{2016E} - \text{Taxes}_{2016E}$$
$$= \$644.6 \text{ million} - \$244.9 \text{ million}$$

a. $222.5 million. 2013 depreciation & amortization is calculated as 2013 sales multiplied by 6%. ($3,708.8 million × 6%)

b. $590.3 million. 2014 EBIT is calculated as 2014 EBITDA less 2014 depreciation & amortization. ($826.1 million - $235.9 million)

c. $235.5 million. 2015 taxes are calculated as 2015 EBIT multiplied by 38%. ($619.8 million × 38%)

d. $399.6 million. 2016 EBIAT is calculated as 2016 EBIT less 2016 taxes. ($644.6 million - $244.9 million)

3) ValueCo's 2011 working capital ratios

ValueCo Corporation
Working Capital Projections
($ in millions, fiscal year ending December 31)

	Historical Period			2012
	2009	2010	2011	
Sales	$2,600.0	$2,900.0	$3,200.0	$3,450.0
Cost of Goods Sold	1,612.0	1,769.0	1,920.0	2,070.0
Current Assets				
Accounts Receivable	317.0	365.5	417.4	450.0
Inventories	441.6	496.8	556.5	600.0
Prepaid Expenses and Other	117.0	142.1	162.3	175.0
Total Current Assets	**$875.6**	**$1,004.4**	**$1,136.2**	**$1,225.0**
Current Liabilities				
Accounts Payable	189.9	189.0	199.4	215.0
Accrued Liabilities	221.0	237.8	255.1	275.0
Other Current Liabilities	75.4	84.1	92.8	100.0
Total Current Liabilities	**$486.3**	**$510.9**	**$547.2**	**$590.0**
Net Working Capital	**$389.4**	**$493.5**	**$589.0**	**$635.0**
% sales	*15.0%*	*17.0%*	*18.4%*	*18.4%*
(Increase)/Decrease in NWC		($104.1)	($95.5)	($46.0)

$= \text{Prepaids and Other Current Assets}_{2011} / \text{Sales}_{2011}$
$= \$162.3 \text{ million} / \$3,200.0 \text{ million}$

$= (\text{Inventories}_{2011} / \text{COGS}_{2011}) \times 365$
$= (\$556.5 \text{ million} / \$1,920.0 \text{ million}) \times 365$

$= (\text{A/R}_{2011} / \text{Sales}_{2011}) \times 365$
$= (\$417.4 \text{ million} / \$3,200.0 \text{ million}) \times 365$

Assumptions

Current Assets				
Days Sales Outstanding	44.5	46.0	47.6	47.6
Days Inventory Held	100.0	102.5	105.8	105.8
Prepaids and Other CA (% of sales)	4.5%	4.9%	5.1%	5.1%
Current Liabilities				
Days Payable Outstanding	43.0	39.0	37.9	37.9
Accrued Liabilities (% of sales)	8.5%	8.2%	8.0%	8.0%
Other Current Liabilities (% of sales)	2.9%	2.9%	2.9%	2.9%

$= \text{Other Current Liabilities}_{2011} / \text{Sales}_{2011}$
$= \$92.8 \text{ million} / \$3,200.0 \text{ million}$

$= \text{Accrued Liabilities}_{2011} / \text{Sales}_{2011}$
$= \$255.1 \text{ million} / \$3,200.0 \text{ million}$

$= (\text{A/P}_{2011} / \text{COGS}_{2011}) \times 365$
$= (\$199.4 \text{ million} / \$1,920.0 \text{ million}) \times 365$

a. 47.6. 2011 days sales outstanding is calculated as 2011 accounts receivable divided by 2011 sales, multiplied by 365. (($417.4 million / $3,200.0 million) × 365)

b. 105.8. 2011 days inventory held is calculated as 2011 inventories divided by 2011 cost of goods sold, multiplied by 365. (($556.5 million / $1,920.0 million) × 365)

c. 5.1%. 2011 prepaids and other current assets as a percentage of sales is calculated as 2011 prepaid expenses and other current assets divided by 2011 sales. ($162.3 million / $3,200.0 million)

d. 37.9. 2011 days payable outstanding is calculated as 2011 accounts payable divided by 2011 cost of goods sold, multiplied by 365. (($199.4 million / $1,920.0 million) × 365)

e. 8.0%. 2011 accrued liabilities as a percentage of sales is calculated as 2011 accrued liabilities divided by 2011 sales. ($255.1 million / $3,200.0 million)

f. 2.9%. 2011 other current liabilities as a percentage of sales is calculated as 2011 other current liabilities divided by 2011 sales. ($92.8 million / $3,200.0 million)

4)   ValueCo's working capital projections

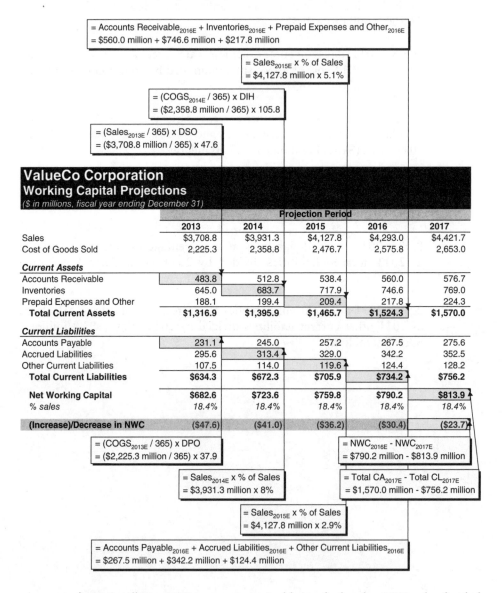

= Accounts Receivable$_{2016E}$ + Inventories$_{2016E}$ + Prepaid Expenses and Other$_{2016E}$
= $560.0 million + $746.6 million + $217.8 million

= Sales$_{2015E}$ x % of Sales
= $4,127.8 million x 5.1%

= (COGS$_{2014E}$ / 365) x DIH
= ($2,358.8 million / 365) x 105.8

= (Sales$_{2013E}$ / 365) x DSO
= ($3,708.8 million / 365) x 47.6

ValueCo Corporation
Working Capital Projections
($ in millions, fiscal year ending December 31)

			Projection Period		
	2013	2014	2015	2016	2017
Sales	$3,708.8	$3,931.3	$4,127.8	$4,293.0	$4,421.7
Cost of Goods Sold	2,225.3	2,358.8	2,476.7	2,575.8	2,653.0
Current Assets					
Accounts Receivable	483.8	512.8	538.4	560.0	576.7
Inventories	645.0	683.7	717.9	746.6	769.0
Prepaid Expenses and Other	188.1	199.4	209.4	217.8	224.3
Total Current Assets	**$1,316.9**	**$1,395.9**	**$1,465.7**	**$1,524.3**	**$1,570.0**
Current Liabilities					
Accounts Payable	231.1	245.0	257.2	267.5	275.6
Accrued Liabilities	295.6	313.4	329.0	342.2	352.5
Other Current Liabilities	107.5	114.0	119.6	124.4	128.2
Total Current Liabilities	**$634.3**	**$672.3**	**$705.9**	**$734.2**	**$756.2**
Net Working Capital	**$682.6**	**$723.6**	**$759.8**	**$790.2**	**$813.9**
% sales	*18.4%*	*18.4%*	*18.4%*	*18.4%*	*18.4%*
(Increase)/Decrease in NWC	**($47.6)**	**($41.0)**	**($36.2)**	**($30.4)**	**($23.7)**

= (COGS$_{2013E}$ / 365) x DPO
= ($2,225.3 million / 365) x 37.9

= NWC$_{2016E}$ - NWC$_{2017E}$
= $790.2 million - $813.9 million

= Sales$_{2014E}$ x % of Sales
= $3,931.3 million x 8%

= Total CA$_{2017E}$ - Total CL$_{2017E}$
= $1,570.0 million - $756.2 million

= Sales$_{2015E}$ x % of Sales
= $4,127.8 million x 2.9%

= Accounts Payable$_{2016E}$ + Accrued Liabilities$_{2016E}$ + Other Current Liabilities$_{2016E}$
= $267.5 million + $342.2 million + $124.4 million

a. $483.8 million. 2013 accounts receivable is calculated as 2013 sales divided
by 365, multiplied by 2013 days sales outstanding. (($3,708.8 million /
365) × 47.6)

b. $683.7 million. 2014 inventories is calculated as 2014 cost of goods sold divided by 365, multiplied by 2014 days inventory held. (($2,358.8 million / 365) × 105.8)

c. $209.4 million. 2015 prepaid expenses and other current assets is calculated as 2015 sales multiplied by 2015 prepaids and other current assets as a percentage of sales. ($4,127.8 million × 5.1%)

d. $1,524.3 million. 2016 total current assets is calculated as the sum of 2016 accounts receivable, inventories, and prepaid expenses and other current assets. ($560.0 million + $746.6 million + $217.8 million)

e. $231.1 million. 2013 accounts payable is calculated as 2013 cost of goods sold divided by 365, multiplied by 2013 days payable outstanding. (($2,225.3 million / 365) × 37.9)

f. $313.4 million. 2014 accrued liabilities is calculated as 2014 sales multiplied by 2014 accrued liabilities as a percentage of sales. ($3,931.3 million × 8.0%)

g. $119.6 million. 2015 other current liabilities is calculated as 2015 sales multiplied by 2015 other current liabilities as a percentage of sales. ($4,127.8 million × 2.9%)

h. $734.2 million. 2016 total current liabilities is calculated as the sum of 2016 accounts payable, accrued liabilities, and other current liabilities. ($267.5 million + $342.2 million + $124.4 million)

i. $813.9 million. 2017 net working capital is calculated as 2017 total assets less 2017 total current liabilities. ($1,570.0 million - $756.2 million)

j. ($23.7) million. 2017 increase/(decrease) in NWC is calculated as 2016 NWC less 2017 net working capital. ($790.2 million - $813.9 million)

5) ValueCo's projected free cash flow

ValueCo Corporation
($ in millions, fiscal year ending December 31)

	Projection Period				
	2013	2014	2015	2016	2017
EBIAT	$345.2	$366.0	$384.3	$399.6	$411.6
Plus: D&A	222.5	235.9	247.7	257.6	265.3
Less: Capex	(166.9)	(176.9)	(185.8)	(193.2)	(199.0)
Less: Inc./(Dec.) in NWC	(47.6)	(41.0)	(36.2)	(30.4)	(23.7)
Unlevered FCF	$353.3	$384.0	$410.0	$433.6	$454.2

= Sales$_{2013E}$ x % of Sales
= $3,708.8 million x 4.5%

= EBIAT$_{2014E}$ + D&A$_{2014E}$ - Capital Expenditures$_{2014E}$ - Increase/(Decrease) in NWC$_{2014E}$
= $366.0 million + $235.9 million - 176.9 million - $41.0 million

a. ($166.9) million. 2013 capex is calculated as 2013 sales multiplied by 4.5%. ($3,708.8 × 4.5%)

b. $384.0 million. 2014 free cash flow is calculated as 2014 EBIAT plus 2014 depreciation & amortization less 2014 capex and 2014 increase/(decrease) in net working capital. ($366.0 million + $235.9 million - $176.9 million - $41.0 million)

6) WACC calculation for ValueCo

a. 70%. Equity-to-total capitalization is calculated as one minus debt-to-total capitalization. (1-30%)

b. 42.9%. Target debt/equity is calculated as debt-to-total capitalization divided by equity-to-total capitalization. (30% / 70%)

c. 3.7%. After-tax cost-of-debt is calculated as the cost-of-debt multiplied by one minus the tax rate. (6% × (1-38%))

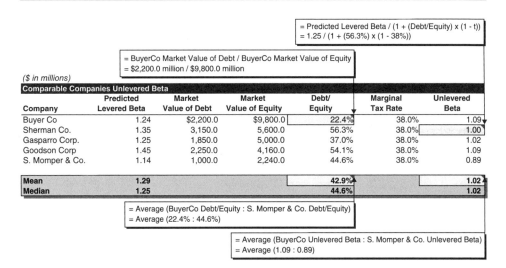

= Predicted Levered Beta / (1 + (Debt/Equity) x (1 - t))
= 1.25 / (1 + (56.3%) x (1 - 38%))

= BuyerCo Market Value of Debt / BuyerCo Market Value of Equity
= $2,200.0 million / $9,800.0 million

($ in millions)

Comparable Companies Unlevered Beta

Company	Predicted Levered Beta	Market Value of Debt	Market Value of Equity	Debt/ Equity	Marginal Tax Rate	Unlevered Beta
Buyer Co	1.24	$2,200.0	$9,800.0	22.4%	38.0%	1.09
Sherman Co.	1.35	3,150.0	5,600.0	56.3%	38.0%	1.00
Gasparro Corp.	1.25	1,850.0	5,000.0	37.0%	38.0%	1.02
Goodson Corp	1.45	2,250.0	4,160.0	54.1%	38.0%	1.09
S. Momper & Co.	1.14	1,000.0	2,240.0	44.6%	38.0%	0.89
Mean	**1.29**			**42.9%**		**1.02**
Median	**1.25**			**44.6%**		**1.02**

= Average (BuyerCo Debt/Equity : S. Momper & Co. Debt/Equity)
= Average (22.4% : 44.6%)

= Average (BuyerCo Unlevered Beta : S. Momper & Co. Unlevered Beta)
= Average (1.09 : 0.89)

d. 22.4%. BuyerCo's debt-to-equity is calculated as the market value of debt divided by the market value of equity. ($2,200.0 million / $9,800.0 million)

e. 1.00. Sherman Co.'s unlevered beta is calculated as shown below:

$$\beta_U = \frac{\beta_L}{\left(1 + \dfrac{D}{E} \times (1-t)\right)}$$

$$1.00 = \frac{1.35}{(1 + 0.56 \times (1 - 0.38))}$$

where: β_U = unlevered beta
  β_L = levered beta
  D/E = debt-to-equity ratio
  t = marginal tax rate

f. 42.9%. The mean debt-to-equity ratio for the comparable companies is calculated by taking the average of the debt-to-equity ratios for the comparable companies.

g. 1.02. The mean unlevered beta for the comparable companies is calculated by taking the average of the unlevered betas for the comparable companies.

h. 1.29. ValueCo's relevered beta is calculated by using the following formula:

$$\beta_L = \beta_U \times \left(1 + \frac{D}{E} \times (1-t)\right)$$

where: D/E = <u>target</u> debt-to-equity ratio

ValueCo Relevered Beta

	Mean Unlevered Beta	Target Debt/ Equity	Target Marginal Tax Rate	Relevered Beta
Relevered Beta	1.02	42.9%	38.0%	1.29

= Average Unlevered Beta x (1 + (Target Debt/Equity) x (1 - Target Marginal Tax Rate)
= 1.02 x (1 + (42.9%) x (1 - 38%))

    i.   12.7%. Cost of equity is calculated by using the following formula:

Cost of Equity (r_e) = Risk-free Rate + Levered Beta x Market Risk Premium

Cost of Equity (r_e) = $r_f + \beta_L \times (r_m - r_f)$

Cost of Equity

Risk-free Rate	3.0%
Market Risk Premium	6.62%
Levered Beta	1.29
Size Premium	1.14%
Cost of Equity	**12.7%**

= Risk-free Rate + (Levered Beta x Market Risk Premium) + Size Premium
= 3% + (1.29 x 6.62%) + 1.14%

    j.   10.0%. Weighted average cost of capital is calculated as shown below:

$$WACC = (r_d \times (1-t)) \times \frac{D}{D+E} + r_e \times \frac{E}{D+E}$$

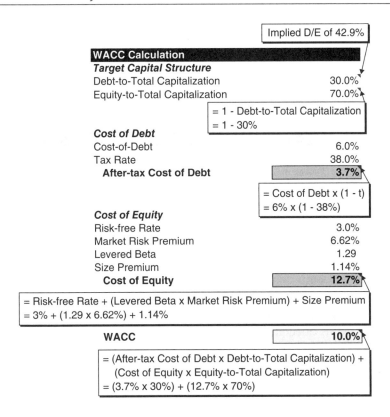

7) ValueCo's terminal value

    a. $6,969.0 million. Terminal value using the exit multiple method is calculated as shown below:

$$\text{Terminal Value} \quad = \quad \boxed{\text{EBITDA}_n \ \times \ \text{Exit Multiple}}$$

where: n = terminal year of the projection period

($ in millions)

Calculation of Terminal Value using EMM	
Terminal Year EBITDA (2017E)	$929.2
Exit Multiple	7.5x
Terminal Value	**$6,969.0**

$= \text{EBITDA}_{\text{Terminal Year}} \times \text{Exit Multiple}$
$= \$929.2 \text{ million} \times 7.5x$

    b. 3.0%. The implied perpetuity growth rate is calculated as shown below:

$$\text{Implied Perpetuity Growth Rate} = \frac{((\text{Terminal Value}^{(a)} \times \text{WACC}) - \text{FCF}_{\text{Terminal Year}} \times (1 + \text{WACC})^{0.5})}{(\text{Terminal Value}^{(a)} + \text{FCF}_{\text{Terminal Year}} \times (1 + \text{WACC})^{0.5})}$$

[a] Terminal Value calculated using the EMM.

($ in millions)

Implied Perpetuity Growth Rate	
Terminal Year Free Cash Flow (2017E)	$454.2
Discount Rate	10.0%
Terminal Value	$6,969.0
Implied Perpetuity Growth Rate	**3.0%**

= ((EMM Terminal Value x WACC) - FCF$_{\text{Terminal Year}}$ x (1 + WACC)$^{0.5}$) /
 (EMM Terminal Value + FCF$_{\text{Terminal Year}}$ x (1 + WACC)$^{0.5}$)

= (($6,969 million) x 10%) - $454.2 million x (1 + 10%)$^{0.5}$) /
 ($6,969 million + $454.2 million x (1 + 10%)$^{0.5}$)

c. $6,683.8 million The terminal value using the perpetuity growth method (PGM) is calculated as shown below:

$$\text{Terminal Value} = \frac{\text{FCF}_n \times (1 + g)}{(r - g)}$$

where: FCF = unlevered free cash flow
　　　　 n = terminal year of the projection period
　　　　 g = perpetuity growth rate
　　　　 r = WACC

($ in millions)

Calculation of Terminal Value using PGM	
Terminal Year Free Cash Flow (2017E)	$454.2
WACC	10.0%
Perpetuity Growth Rate	3.0%
Terminal Value	**$6,683.8**

= FCF$_{\text{Terminal Year}}$ x (1 + Perpetuity Growth Rate) / (WACC - Perpetuity Growth Rate)
= $454.2 million x (1 + 3%) / (10% - 3%)

d. 7.5x. The implied exit multiple is calculated as shown below:

$$\text{Implied Exit Multiple} = \frac{\text{Terminal Value}^{(a)} \times (1 + \text{WACC})^{0.5}}{\text{EBITDA}_{\text{Terminal Year}}}$$

[a] Terminal Value calculated using the PGM.

($ in millions)

Implied Exit Multiple	
Terminal Value	$6,683.8
Terminal Year EBITDA (2017E)	929.2
WACC	10.0%
Implied Exit Multiple	**7.5x**

= PGM Terminal Value x $(1 + WACC)^{0.5}$ / $EBITDA_{Terminal\ Year}$
= $6,683.8 million x $(1 + 10\%)^{0.5}$ / $929.2 million

8) Present value calculation

= 1 / $((1 + WACC)^{(n - .05)})$
= 1 / $((1 + 10\%)^{(1.5)})$
Note: Mid-Year Convention

= Current Year - Year 0 - 0.5
= 2013 - 2012 - 0.5
Note: Mid-Year Convention applied

($ in millions)

Present Value Calculation

		Projection Period				
		2013	2014	2015	2016	2017
Unlevered Free Cash Flow		$353.3	$384.0	$410.0	$433.6	$454.2
WACC	10.0%					
Discount Period		0.5	1.5	2.5	3.5	4.5
Discount Factor		0.95	0.87	0.79	0.72	0.65
Present Value of Free Cash Flow		**$336.8**	**$332.8**	**$323.1**	**$310.6**	**$295.8**

= Unlevered FCF_{2015E} x Discount Factor
= $410.0 million x 0.79

Terminal Value

Terminal Year EBITDA (2017E)	$929.2
Exit Multiple	7.5x
Terminal Value	**$6,969.0**
Discount Factor	0.62
Present Value of Terminal Value	**$4,327.2**

= Terminal Value x Discount Factor
= $6,969.0 million x 0.62

= 1 / $((1 + WACC)^{n})$
= 1 / $((1 + 10\%)^{5})$
Note: Mid-Year Convention not applied for Exit Multiple Method

a. 0.5. 2013 discount period is calculated as the current year less Year 0 less 0.5. (2013 - 2012 - 0.5)

b. 0.87. 2014 discount factor is calculated as shown below:

$$\text{Discount Factor} = \frac{1}{(1 + \text{WACC})^{(n - 0.5)}}$$

$$0.87 = \frac{\$1.00}{(1 + 10\%)^{1.5}}$$

c. \$323.1 million. 2015 present value of free cash flow is calculated as 2015 free cash flow multiplied by 2015 discount factor. (\$410.0 million × 0.79)

d. 0.62. The terminal value discount factor is calculated as shown below:

$$\text{Discount Factor} = \frac{1}{(1 + \text{WACC})^{(\text{Terminal Year})}}$$

$$0.62 = \frac{\$1.00}{(1 + 10\%)^{5}}$$

e. \$4,327.2 million. The present value of the terminal value is calculated as the terminal value multiplied by the terminal value discount factor. (\$6,969.0 million × 0.62)

9) ValueCo's enterprise value

($ in millions)	
Enterprise Value	
Cumulative Present Value of FCF	**$1,599.2**
Terminal Value	
Terminal Year EBITDA (2017E)	$929.2
Exit Multiple	7.5x
Terminal Value	**$6,969.0**
Discount Factor	0.62
Present Value of Terminal Value	**$4,327.2**
% of Enterprise Value	73.0%
Enterprise Value	**$5,926.4**

= Sum (FCF$_{2013E-2017E,}$ discounted at 10%)
= Sum ($336.8 million : $295.8 million)

= PV of FCF$_{2013-2017}$ + PV of Terminal Value
= $1,599.2 million + $4,327.2 million

= PV of Terminal Value / Enterprise Value
= $4,327.2 million / $5,926.4 million

a. $1,599.2 million. The cumulative present value of FCF is calculated as the sum of the present value of free cash flows from 2013 through 2017.

b. $5,926.4 million. The enterprise value is calculated as the cumulative present value of FCF plus the present value of terminal value. ($1,599.2 million + $4,327.2 million)

c. 73.0%. The percentage of enterprise value represented by the terminal value is calculated as the present value of terminal value divided by the enterprise value. ($4,327.2 million / $5,926.4 million)

10) ValueCo's equity value and implied share price

($ in millions)	
Implied Equity Value and Share Price	
Enterprise Value	$5,926.4
Less: Total Debt	(1,500.0)
Less: Preferred Stock	-
Less: Noncontrolling Interest	-
Plus: Cash and Cash Equivalents	250.0
Implied Equity Value	**$4,676.4**

= Enterprise Value - Total Debt + Cash and Cash Equivalents
= $5,926.4 million - $1,500.0 million + $250.0 million

> = Exercise Price x In-the-Money Shares
> = $45.00 x 0.750 million

> = IF (Exercise Price < Implied Share Price, then
> display Number of Shares, otherwise display 0)
> = IF ($25.00 < $57.10, 2.25, 0)

($ in millions, except per share data)

Calculation of Implied Share Price	
Enterprise Value	$5,926.4
Less: Total Debt	(1,500.0)
Plus: Cash and Cash Equivalents	250.0
Implied Equity Value	**$4,676.4**

Options/Warrants

Tranche	Number of Shares	Exercise Price	In-the-Money Shares	Proceeds
Tranche 1	2.250	$25.00	2.250	56.3
Tranche 2	1.000	30.00	1.000	30.0
Tranche 3	0.750	45.00	0.750	33.8
Tranche 4	0.500	57.50	-	-
Tranche 5	0.250	75.00	-	-
Total	**4.750**		**4.000**	**$120.0**

Basic Shares Outstanding	80.000
Plus: Shares from In-the-Money Options	4.000
Less: Shares Repurchased	(2.102)
Net New Shares from Options	**1.898**
Plus: Shares from Convertible Securities	-
Fully Diluted Shares Outstanding	**81.898**

Implied Share Price	**$57.10**

> = Implied Equity Value / Fully Diluted Shares
> = $4.7 billion / 81.898 million

> = - Total Option Proceeds / Implied Share Price
> = ($120.0) million / $57.10

a. $4,676.4 million. The implied equity value is calculated as the enterprise value less total debt plus cash and cash equivalents. ($5,926.4 million - $1,500 million + $250 million)

b. 81.898 million. The existence of in-the-money options and warrants, creates a circular reference in the basic formula shown below:

$$\text{Implied Share Price} = \frac{\text{Implied Equity Value}}{\text{Fully Diluted Shares Outstanding}}$$

In other words, equity value per share is dependent on the number of fully diluted shares outstanding, which, in turn, is dependent on the implied share price. As shown below, this is remedied in the model by activating the iteration function in Microsoft Excel.

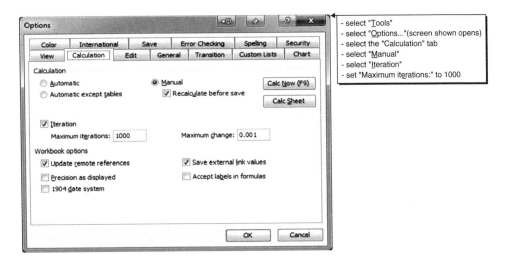

As shown above, 4 million shares are in the money as their exercise prices are below the implied share price of $57.10. Under the TSM, it is assumed that the proceeds received from the options exercise are used to repurchase shares at an implied share price of $57.10. Therefore, the company repurchases 2.102 million shares, resulting in 1.898 million net new shares which are added to the company's basis shares outstanding to derive fully diluted shares of 81.198 million.

c. $57.10. Implied equity value is divided by the company's fully diluted shares outstanding to calculate an implied share price.

11) B. The correct order is:

    I. Study the Target and Determine Key Performance Drivers
    II. Project Free Cash Flow
    III. Calculate Weighted Average Cost of Capital
    IV. Determine Terminal Value
    V. Calculate Present Value and Determine Valuation

12) D. Prepaid expenses, which are payments made by a company before a product has been delivered or a service has been performed, are current assets. The other choices are long-term assets or liabilities.

13) A. Goodwill, which is the value paid in excess over the book value of an asset, is a long-term asset. The other choices are short-term assets and liabilities.

14) C. FCF is the cash generated by a company after paying all cash operating expenses and associated taxes, as well as the funding of capital expenditures and working capital, but prior to the payment of any interest expense.

($ in millions)

Free Cash Flow Calculation	
EBIT	$300.0
Taxes	114.0
EBIAT	**$186.0**
Plus: Depreciation & Amortization	50.0
Less: Capital Expenditures	(25.0)
Less: Inc./(Dec.) in Net Working Capital	(10.0)
Unlevered Free Cash Flow	**$201.0**

= EBIAT + Depreciation & Amortization - Capital Expenditures
 - Inc./(Dec.) in Net Working Capital
= $186.0 million + $50.0 million - $25.0 million - $10.0 million

15) A. See calculation below:

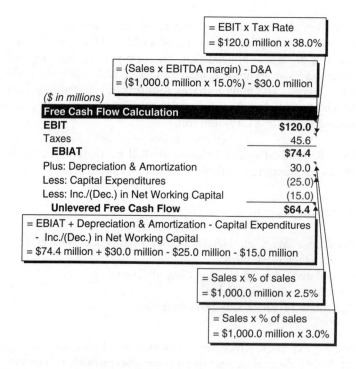

= EBIT x Tax Rate
= $120.0 million x 38.0%

= (Sales x EBITDA margin) - D&A
= ($1,000.0 million x 15.0%) - $30.0 million

($ in millions)

Free Cash Flow Calculation	
EBIT	$120.0
Taxes	45.6
EBIAT	**$74.4**
Plus: Depreciation & Amortization	30.0
Less: Capital Expenditures	(25.0)
Less: Inc./(Dec.) in Net Working Capital	(15.0)
Unlevered Free Cash Flow	**$64.4**

= EBIAT + Depreciation & Amortization - Capital Expenditures
 - Inc./(Dec.) in Net Working Capital
= $74.4 million + $30.0 million - $25.0 million - $15.0 million

= Sales x % of sales
= $1,000.0 million x 2.5%

= Sales x % of sales
= $1,000.0 million x 3.0%

16) C. Historical growth rates, EBIT margins, and other ratios can be a reliable indicator of future performance, especially for mature companies in

non-cyclical sectors. Typically, the prior three-year period (if available) serves as a good proxy for projecting future financial performance.

17)   C. Typically, FCF is projected for a period of five years, but is dependent on the target's sector, stage of development, and the predictability of its financial performance. It is critical to project FCF to a point in the future where the target's financial performance reaches a normalized level. For mature companies in established industries, five years is often sufficient for allowing a company to reach its steady state and usually spans at least one business cycle.

18)   D. In a DCF, a company's FCF is typically projected for a period of five years. The projection period, however, may be longer depending on the company's sector, business model, stage of development, and the underlying predictability of its financial performance.

19)   A. It may be appropriate to use a 15 to 20 year projection period for companies with highly predictable or contracted revenue streams.

20)   A. Utility companies typically have highly predictable or contracted revenue streams and can have a longer projection period than five years.

21)   C. WACC, exit multiple, and EBIT margins are commonly sensitized in the DCF. Other variables that are often sensitized include perpetuity growth rate and sales growth rates.

22)   B. Mining companies, heavy equipment manufactures and oil and gas companies typically have high capital expenditures. Capital expenditures, which are funds that a company uses to purchase, improve, expand, or replace physical assets, are capitalized on the balance sheet once the expenditure is made and then expensed over its useful life as depreciation through the company's income statement.

23)   D. Capital expenditures, sales growth, EBIT margins as well as depreciation and amortization and increase / (decrease) in net working capital are key drivers of a company's projected FCF.

24)   A. Beta is a measure of the covariance between the rate of return on a company's stock and the overall market return (systematic risk), with the S&P 500 traditionally used as a proxy for the market. As the S&P 500 has a beta of 1.0,

a stock with a beta of 1.0 should have an expected return equal to that of the market.

25) A. CAPM is based on the premise that equity investors need to be compensated for their assumption of systematic risk in the form of a risk premium, or the amount of market return in excess of a stated risk-free rate. Systematic risk is the risk related to the overall market, which is also known as non-diversifiable risk.

26) B. A stock with a beta of less than 1.0 has lower systematic risk than the market, and a stock with a beta greater than 1.0 has higher systematic risk. Mathematically, this is captured in the CAPM, with a higher beta stock exhibiting a higher cost of equity; and vice versa for lower beta stocks.

27) D. When there is no debt in the capital structure, WACC is equal to the cost of equity.

28) A. Depreciation and amortization (D&A) are both non-cash expenses and reduce reported earnings. They reduce the value of capitalized assets over an estimated useful life and are explicitly disclosed in the cash flow statement.

29) B. Capital expenditures, as opposed to depreciation, represent actual cash outflows and, consequently, must be subtracted from EBIAT in the calculation of FCF.

30) D. The calculation to determine the increase or decrease in net working capital from 2012 to 2013 is found by subtracting 2012 net working capital from 2013 net working capital.

($ in millions)

Net Working Capital Calculation		
	2012	**2013**
Current Assets		
Accounts Receivable	325.0	350.0
Inventories	200.0	210.0
Prepaid Expenses and Other	35.0	45.0
Total Current Assets	**$560.0**	**$605.0**
Current Liabilities		
Accounts Payable	300.0	315.0
Accrued Liabilities	150.0	160.0
Other Current Liabilities	60.0	65.0
Total Current Liabilities	**$510.0**	**$540.0**
Net Working Capital	**$50.0**	**$65.0**
(Increase) / Decrease in NWC		**($15.0)**

$$= NWC_{2012E} - NWC_{2013E}$$
$$= \$50.0 \text{ million} - \$65.0 \text{ million}$$

31) A. When a current asset (e.g. accounts receivable, inventory) increases, it is considered a use of cash. When a current asset decreases, it is considered a source of cash.

32) B. When a current liability (e.g. accounts payable, accrued liabilities) increases, it is considered a source of cash. When a current liability decreases, it is considered a use of cash.

33) A. DSO provides a gauge of how well a company is managing the collection of its A/R by measuring the number of days it takes to collect payment after the sale of a product or service. The lower a company's DSO, the faster it receives cash from credit sales.

34) C. DSO is calculated by dividing accounts receivable by sales, and multiplying the answer by 365 (days).

$$DSO = \frac{A/R}{Sales} \times 365$$

$$31 \text{ days} = \frac{\$300 \text{ million}}{\$3,500 \text{ million}} \times 365$$

35) D. DIH measures the number of days it takes a company to sell its inventory. An increase in inventory represents a use of cash. Therefore, companies strive to minimize DIH and turn their inventory as quickly as possible so as to minimize the amount of cash it ties up.

36) C. Inventory turns measures the number of times a company turns over its inventory in a given year.

37) C. DIH is calculated by dividing inventory by COGS, and multiplying the answer by 365 (days).

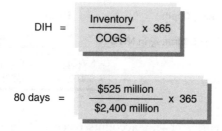

$$DIH = \frac{Inventory}{COGS} \times 365$$

$$80 \text{ days} = \frac{\$525 \text{ million}}{\$2,400 \text{ million}} \times 365$$

38) A. Inventory turns ratio, an alternate approach for measuring a company's efficiency at selling its inventory, is calculated by dividing COGS by inventory.

$$Inventory \ Turns = COGS / Inventory$$

$$4.6x = \$2,400 \text{ million} / \$525 \text{ million}$$

39) D. DPO measures the number of days it takes for a company to make payment on its outstanding purchases of goods and services. The higher a company's DPO, the more time it has available to use its cash on hand for various business purposes before paying outstanding bills.

40) A. DPO is calculated by dividing accounts payable by COGS, and multiplying the answer by 365 (days).

$$\text{DPO} = \frac{\text{A/P}}{\text{COGS}} \times 365$$

$$28 \text{ days} = \frac{\$250 \text{ million}}{\$3,300 \text{ million}} \times 365$$

41) B. Cost of equity is the required annual rate of return that a company's equity investors expect to receive (including dividends). To calculate the expected return on a company's equity, employ the capital asset pricing model (CAPM).

42) C. Investment banks may differ on accepted proxies for the appropriate risk-free rate, with many using the yield on the 10-year U.S. Treasury note and others preferring the yield on longer-term Treasuries. The general goal is to use as long-dated an instrument as possible to match the expected life of the company (assuming a going concern), but practical considerations also need to be taken into account. Ibbotson Associates ("Ibbotson") uses an interpolated yield for a 20-year bond as the basis for the risk-free rate.

43) C. The market risk premium is the spread of the expected market return over the risk-free rate. Finance professionals typically use Ibbotson to track data on the equity risk premium. According to Ibbotson, for the 1926-2012 time period, the market risk premium is approximately 6.62%.

44) A. As shown below, to calculate the cost of equity using CAPM, multiply the levered beta by the market risk premium and then take this product and add the risk-free rate.

$$\text{Cost of Equity } (r_e) = \text{Risk-free Rate} + \text{Levered Beta} \times \text{Market Risk Premium}$$

$$11.3\% = 3.0\% + 1.25 \times 6.6\%$$

45) B. Companies in the social media, homebuilder, and chemicals sector are more volatile and riskier than companies in the utility sector. Therefore, a utility company should have a lower beta.

46) B. See calculation below:

$$\beta_U = \frac{\beta_L}{\left(1 + \dfrac{D}{E} \times (1-t)\right)}$$

$$1.00 = \frac{1.25}{\left(1 + 0.40 \times (1 - 0.38)\right)}$$

where: β_U = unlevered beta
β_L = levered beta
D/E = debt-to-equity ratio
t = marginal tax rate

47) C. See calculation below:

$$\beta_L = \beta_U \times \left(1 + \frac{D}{E} \times (1-t)\right)$$

$$1.28 = 1.00 \times \left(1 + 0.45 \times (1 - 0.38)\right)$$

where: D/E = <u>target</u> debt-to-equity ratio

48) C. The DCF approach to valuation is based on determining the present value of all future FCF produced by a company. As it is infeasible to project a company's FCF indefinitely, a terminal value is used to determine the value of the company beyond the projection period.

49) B. The PGM calculates terminal value by treating a company's terminal year FCF as a perpetuity growing at an assumed rate. As shown below, this method relies on the WACC calculation and requires an assumption regarding the company's long-term, sustainable growth rate ("perpetuity growth rate").

$$\text{Terminal Value} = \frac{FCF_n \times (1 + g)}{(r - g)}$$

$$\$2{,}861.1 \text{ million} = \frac{\$250 \text{ million} \times (1 + 3\%)}{(12\% - 3\%)}$$

where: FCF = unlevered free cash flow
n = terminal year of the projection period
g = perpetuity growth rate
r = WACC

50)   A. The use of a mid-year convention results in a slightly higher valuation than year-end discounting due to the fact that FCF is received sooner.

51)   D. See calculation below:

$$\text{Discount Factor} = \frac{1}{(1 + WACC)^{(n - 0.5)}}$$

$$\$472.5 \text{ million} = \frac{\$500 \text{ million}}{(1 + 12\%)^{0.5}}$$

where: n = year in the projection period
0.5 = is subtracted from n in accordance with a mid-year convention

52)   A. When employing a mid-year convention for the projection period, mid-year discounting is also applied for the terminal value under the PGM, as the calculation is discounting perpetual future FCF assumed to be received throughout the year. The EMM, however, which is typically based on the LTM trading multiples of comparable companies for a calendar year end EBITDA (or EBIT), uses year-end discounting.

53)   C. See calculation below:

> = 1 / ((1 + WACC)^(n - .05)
> = 1 / ((1 + 10.0%)^(4.5))
> Note: Mid-Year Convention applied

($ in millions)

Present Value Calculation

		Projection Period				
		2013	2014	2015	2016	2017
Unlevered Free Cash Flow		$100.0	$110.0	$120.0	$125.0	$130.0
WACC	10.0%					
Discount Period		0.5	1.5	2.5	3.5	4.5
Discount Factor		0.95	0.87	0.79	0.72	0.65
Present Value of Free Cash Flow		$95.3	$95.3	$94.6	$89.5	$84.7

> = Unlevered FCF$_{2013E}$ x Discount Factor
> = $100.0 million x 0.95

> = Exit Year EBITDA x Exit Multiple
> = $250.0 million x 7.5x

Terminal Value

Terminal Year EBITDA (2017E)	$250.0
Exit Multiple	7.5x
Terminal Value	**$1,875.0**
Discount Factor	0.62
Present Value of Terminal Value	**$1,164.2**

> = 1 / ((1 + WACC)^n)
> = 1 / ((1 + 10.0%)^5)
> Note: Mid-Year Convention not applied for Exit Multiple Method

($ in millions)

Enterprise Value

Present Value of Free Cash Flow	$459.5

> = SUM (FCF$_{2013E-2017E}$, discounted at 10.0%)
> = SUM ($95.3 million : $84.7 million)

Terminal Value	
Terminal Year EBITDA (2017E)	$250.0
Exit Multiple	7.5x
Terminal Value	**$1,875.0**
Discount Factor	0.62
Present Value of Terminal Value	**$1,164.2**
% of Enterprise Value	71.7%
Enterprise Value	**$1,623.7**

> = Terminal Value x Discount Factor
> = $1,875.0 million x 0.62

> = PV of Terminal Value / Enterprise Value
> = $1,164.2 million / $1,623.7 million

> = PV of FCF$_{2013E-2017E}$ + PV of Terminal Value
> = $459.5 million + $1,164.2 million

$$\text{Discount Factor} = \frac{1}{(1 + WACC)^{(n - 0.5)}}$$

$$0.95 = \frac{\$1.00}{(1 + 10\%)^{0.5}}$$

where: n = year in the projection period
         0.5 = is subtracted from n in accordance with a mid-year convention

54) A. If there are no relevant comparable companies to determine an exit multiple, PGM can be utilized to calculate a terminal value. The PGM is often used in conjunction with the EMM, with each serving as a sanity check on the other.

55) C. In both terminal value formulas, a steady state is required otherwise the terminal value will be skewed.

56) C. A preferred approach in these instances is to approximate a company's cost of debt based on its current (or implied) credit ratings at the target capital structure and the cost of debt for comparable credits, typically with guidance from an in-house DCM professional.

57) B. The use of a terminal value is considered a potential weakness. It is very sensitive to the inputs of the user and can represent 75% or more of the DCF valuation.

58) A. The concept of a size premium is based on empirical evidence suggesting that smaller sized companies are riskier and, therefore, should have a higher cost of equity. This phenomenon, which to some degree contradicts the CAPM, relies on the notion that smaller companies' risk is not entirely captured in their betas given limited trading volumes of their stock, making covariance calculations inexact. As shown below, a size premium can be added to the CAPM formula for smaller companies to account for the perceived higher risk.

$$r_e = r_f + \beta_L \times (r_m - r_f) + SP$$

where: SP = size premium

59) For a highly cyclical business such as a steel or lumber company sales levels need to track the movements of the underlying commodity cycle. Consequently, sales trends are typically more volatile and may incorporate dramatic peak-to-trough swings depending on the company's point in the cycle at the start of the projection period.

60) Regardless of where in the cycle the projection period begins, it is crucial that the terminal year financial performance represents a normalized level as opposed to a cyclical high or low. Otherwise, the company's terminal value, which usually comprises a substantial portion of the overall value in a DCF, will be skewed toward an unrepresentative level.

61) On the income statement, depreciation is sometimes broken out as a separate line item, but generally included in COGS. On the cash flow statement, it is added back to net income under cash flow from operating activities. Finally, on the balance sheet, it is subtracted from the beginning PP&E balance.

62) The enterprise value will decrease. The weighted average cost of capital is a weighted average of the company's cost of debt (tax-effected) and cost of equity based on an assumed or "target" capital structure. As the cost of debt and cost of equity increase, future cash flows and the terminal value are discounted using a larger number.

63) Using a market risk premium of 5.0% vs. 8.0% would result in a higher valuation. A higher discount rate (higher opportunity cost of capital) results in a lower valuation.

64) Benefits of using DCF analysis:

- *Cash flow-based* – reflects value of projected FCF, which represents a more fundamental approach to valuation than using multiples-based methodologies

- *Market independent* – more insulated from market aberrations such as bubbles and distressed periods

- *Self-sufficient* – does not rely entirely upon truly comparable companies or transactions, which may or may not exist, to frame valuation; a DCF is particularly important when there are limited or no "pure play" public comparables to the company being valued

- *Flexibility* – allows the banker to run multiple financial performance scenarios, including improving or declining growth rates, margins, capex requirements, and working capital efficiency

65) Considerations when using DCF analysis:

- *Dependence on financial projections* – accurate forecasting of financial performance is challenging, especially as the projection period lengthens

- *Sensitivity to assumptions* – relatively small changes in key assumptions, such as growth rates, margins, WACC, or exit multiple, can produce meaningfully different valuation ranges

- *Terminal value* – the present value of the terminal value can represent as much as three-quarters or more of the DCF valuation, which decreases the relevance of the projection period's annual FCF

- *Assumes constant capital structure* – basic DCF does not provide flexibility to change the company's capital structure over the projection period

CHAPTER 4

Leveraged Buyouts

1) All of the following are typical "financial sponsors" EXCEPT

    A. Private equity firm
    B. Commercial bank
    C. Hedge fund
    D. Venture capital firm

2) Which of the following are third-party investors that provide financial sponsors with investment capital?

    I. Pension funds
    II. Insurance companies
    III. University endowments
    IV. Wealthy families

    A. I and II
    B. I and III
    C. I, III, and IV
    D. I, II, III, and IV

3) Which of the following is NOT part of an investment bank's financing commitment?

    A. Commitment letter
    B. Institutional letter
    C. Engagement letter
    D. Fee letter

4) Bank lenders consist of all of the following EXCEPT

    A. Commercial banks
    B. Loan mutual funds
    C. Equity asset managers
    D. Credit hedge funds

5) Bond investors consist of all of the following EXCEPT

   A. Hedge funds
   B. Insurance companies
   C. Distressed debt funds
   D. REITs

6) A confidential information memorandum (CIM) for a credit facility contains all of the following EXCEPT

   A. Investment highlights
   B. Projected financials
   C. Description of Notes
   D. Industry overview

7) In which manner does target company management provide tangible value in an LBO?

   A. Helping to achieve favorable financing terms
   B. Ability to draft a quality 10-K
   C. Knowledge of IPO process
   D. Management only provides intangible benefits

8) All of the following are reasons for a public company to consider a take-private LBO EXCEPT

   A. Onerous Sarbanes-Oxley requirements
   B. Access to equity capital markets
   C. Belief that the public market is undervaluing the company
   D. Belief that public ownership is too onerous

9) Which of the following would be potential LBO candidates?

   I. Troubled companies
   II. Companies in fragmented markets
   III. Solid performing companies
   IV. Non-core subsidiaries

   A. III and IV
   B. I, II, and III
   C. II, III, and IV
   D. I, II, III, and IV

10) The ability to maximize leverage in an LBO transaction is facilitated for a company with which of the following characteristics?

    A. Track record for bolt-on acquisitions
    B. Tight covenant package
    C. Strong asset base
    D. Large debt balance

11) What characteristics do sponsors look for when evaluating the management team of an LBO candidate?

    I. Track record of consummating accretive acquisitions
    II. Past experience with a leveraged capital structure
    III. Substantial prior compensation
    IV. History of implementing poison pills

    A. I and II
    B. I and III
    C. II, III, and IV
    D. I, II, III, and IV

12) Which of the following are common exit strategies for financial sponsors?

    I. Refinancing
    II. IPO
    III. Sale to a strategic buyer
    IV. Sale to another sponsor

    A. II and IV
    B. I, II, and III
    C. I, III, and IV
    D. II, III, and IV

13) Which of the following is NOT a typical means for a sponsor to achieve multiple expansion upon exit of its investment?

    A. Increasing the size and scale of the business
    B. Entering into new high growth segments
    C. Efficiency enhancements
    D. Adding overhead

14) What percent of a sponsor's existing equity ownership in the target is kept following a dividend recapitalization?

A. 50%
B. 80%
C. 90%
D. 100%

15) Which of the following is a weakness of a dividend recapitalization?

A. Less sponsor equity
B. Adds additional leverage
C. Cash return
D. Sponsor retains existing equity ownership

16) What is the incentive to take an LBO company public if it does not provide the sponsor with a full exit?

A. Provides sponsors with partial monetization while preserving potential future upside
B. Current M&A markets may be offering high valuation premiums
C. Forced to do so under LP agreements
D. Forced to do so under GP agreements

17) All of the following are advantages to the financial sponsor for taking an LBO target public EXCEPT

A. Provides future upside though residual equity ownership in the target
B. Preserves flexibility to sell at a premium in the future
C. Ease and certainty of execution
D. Potential valuation premium to a M&A sale

18) What is the correct order of seniority for the financing sources listed below from most senior to lease senior?

  I. Equity
 II. Senior subordinated debt
III. First lien secured debt
 IV. Senior unsecured debt

A. II, I, IV, and III
B. III, IV, II, and I
C. III, IV, I, and II
D. IV, III, II, and I

19) Which of the following is NOT a common use of a revolving credit facility?

    A. Maintenance capex
    B. Funding a portion of the LBO purchase price
    C. Working capital
    D. Long-term capital investment

20) Under normal market conditions, the commitment fee on a revolving credit facility is typically set at

    A. 5 bps
    B. 50 bps
    C. 200 bps
    D. 500 bps

21) If a funded revolver is used as part of the LBO financing, how does the coupon compare to other debt instruments in the new capital structure?

    A. Most expensive
    B. Least expensive
    C. Pari passi with the senior notes
    D. Cannot be used as a form of LBO financing

22) ABL facilities are generally secured by

    A. Current assets
    B. Current liabilities
    C. Long-term debt
    D. Pension assets

23) Which of the following is the most likely term loan A lender?

    A. Company executive
    B. Commercial bank
    C. Mezzanine fund
    D. Equity asset manager

24) From the perspective of a financial sponsor, which of the following is a weakness of using high yield bonds as part of LBO financing?

   A. Call protection
   B. Light covenants
   C. Longer tenor
   D. Bullet amortization

25) The tenor of a bridge loan is typically

   A. 1 year
   B. 3 years
   C. 5 years
   D. 10 years

26) On average, what percentage of an LBO financing is funded by the sponsor's equity contribution?

   A. 10%
   B. 30%
   C. 70%
   D. 90%

27) Which of the following is NOT considered collateral by lenders?

   A. Accounts payable
   B. Accounts receivable
   C. Stock
   D. PP&E

28) Which of the following is the correct order of the debt instruments listed below by seniority? Assume 100% of the borrower's assets/collateral are held at the OpCo.

   I. Senior unsecured notes at OpCo
   II. Senior discount notes at HoldCo
   III. First lien secured debt at OpCo
   IV. Second lien secured debt at OpCo

   A. II, I, III, and IV
   B. II, III, IV, and I
   C. III, IV, I, and II
   D. IV, III, I, and II

29) Rank in ascending order the following debt instruments in terms of maturity

    I. Revolver
    II. Senior subordinated notes
    III. Senior notes
    IV. Term loan B

    A. I, IV, III, and II
    B. I, III, II, and IV
    C. IV, III, I, and II
    D. IV, III, II, and I

30) Call protection mitigates which type of risk for debt investors when interest rates are declining?

    A. Credit risk
    B. Operational risk
    C. Reinvestment risk
    D. Extension risk

31) Which of the following is NOT a covenant classification?

    A. Financial
    B. Limitation
    C. Negative
    D. Affirmative

32) Financial maintenance covenants are typical for _____, while _____ typically have incurrence covenants.

    A. Public companies; private companies
    B. Private companies; public companies
    C. High yield bonds; bank debt
    D. Bank debt; high yield bonds

33) Which one of the following is NOT a financial maintenance covenant?

    A. Maximum total leverage
    B. Maximum senior secured leverage
    C. Minimum dividend payments
    D. Minimum interest coverage

34) Which of the following would NOT be classified as a qualified institutional buyer?

   A. Retail investor with under $25 million in net worth
   B. Equity asset manager with $200 million under management
   C. Insurance company with $500 million in investments
   D. Mutual funds with $10,000 million under management

35) With financial maintenance covenants, leverage ratios typically _____ throughout the life of the loan, while coverage ratios typically _____.

   A. Stay constant; increase
   B. Stay constant; decrease
   C. Decrease; increase
   D. Increase; decrease

36) What is the current yield of a $1,000 bond (face value) with a coupon of 6.0% that is trading at par?

   A. 3.0%
   B. 6.0%
   C. 6.3%
   D. 6.5%

37) What is the current yield on a bond trading at $95 that was issued at par with a 7.0% coupon rate?

   A. 7.0%
   B. 7.2%
   C. 7.4%
   D. 7.7%

38) What percent of committed funds do limited partners typically pay general partners as a management fee?

   A. 2%
   B. 5%
   C. 15%
   D. 20%

39) Bonds issued by corporations typically pay interest payments

    A. Monthly
    B. Quarterly
    C. Semiannually
    D. Yearly

40) Which of the following is NOT an advantage of using a revolver?

    A. Shorter maturity compared to other institutional types of debt
    B. Can be drawn, paid down, and redrawn freely during its maturity
    C. Low interest rate
    D. Issued by "relationship" oriented commercial banks

41) Which of the following has the largest impact on LBO valuation?

    A. Entry and exit multiple
    B. Tax rate
    C. Interest rate of debt
    D. Bond non-call period

42) What are the legal documents governing bank debt and bonds, respectively?

    A. Credit agreement; definitive agreement
    B. Indenture; credit agreement
    C. Credit agreement; indenture
    D. Indenture; definitive agreement

43) Which of the following are desirable characteristics for traditional LBO candidates?

    I. Strong market positions
    II. High cyclicality
    III. Large asset base
    IV. Speculative business model

    A. I and II
    B. I and III
    C. II and III
    D. III and IV

44) Are the following types of debt typically secured or unsecured in an LBO capital structure?

High yield bonds	
Revolving credit facility	
Term loan	
Mezzanine debt	
Equity	
ABL facility	

45) Why is a dollar of sustainable EBITDA growth generally favorable to a dollar of debt reduction?

_____

_____

_____

_____

46) What are the potential advantages of a sale vs. an IPO?

_____

_____

_____

_____

47) Describe some of the strategies used to drive multiple expansion?

_____

_____

_____

_____

48) Provide two examples of standard financial maintenance covenants found in credit agreements

_____

_____

49) Draw a diagram explaining *contractual* subordination

50) Draw a diagram explaining *structural* subordination

1) B. A "financial sponsor" refers to traditional private equity (PE) firms, merchant banking divisions of investment banks, hedge funds, venture capital funds, and special purpose acquisition companies (SPACs), among other investment vehicles.

2) D. Third party investors that invest money with PE firms include public and corporate pension funds, insurance companies, endowments and foundations, sovereign wealth funds, and wealthy families/individuals. Sponsor partners and investment professionals may also invest their own money in particular investment opportunities.

3) B. An investment bank's financing commitment includes:

   ▪ *Commitment letter* for the bank debt and a bridge facility (to be provided by the lender in lieu of a bond financing if the capital markets are not available at the time the acquisition is consummated)

   ▪ *Engagement letter* for the investment banks to underwrite the bonds on behalf of the issuer

   ▪ *Fee letter* which sets forth the various fees to be paid to the investment banks in connection with the financing

4) C. Bank lenders typically consist of commercial banks, savings and loan institutions, finance companies, and the investment banks serving as arrangers. The institutional lender base, however, is largely comprised of hedge funds, pension funds, prime funds, insurance companies, and structured vehicles.

5) D. Bond investors are the purchasers of the high yield bonds issued as part of the LBO financing structure. They include high yield mutual funds, hedge funds, pension funds, insurance companies, and distressed debt funds.

6) C. A CIM is a comprehensive document that contains a detailed description of the respective transaction, investment highlights, company, and sector, as well as preliminary term sheets and historical and projected financials. A Description of Notes is found in an indenture for a high yield bond.

7) A. During an LBO process, a strong management team can create tangible value by driving favorable financing terms and pricing, as well as providing sponsors with comfort to stretch on valuation.

8) B. Public companies & management may be motivated to do an LBO by the belief that the market is undervaluing the company, SEC and Sarbanes-Oxley (SOX) compliance is too burdensome and costly (especially for smaller companies), and/or the company could operate more efficiently as a private entity.

9) D. LBO candidates are identified among non-core or underperforming divisions of larger companies, neglected or troubled companies with turnaround potential, or companies in fragmented markets as platforms for a roll-up strategy. Additionally, a potential LBO candidate is simply a solidly performing company with a compelling business model, defensible competitive position, and strong growth opportunities. For a publicly traded LBO candidate, a sponsor may perceive the target as undervalued by the market or recognize opportunities for growth and efficiency not being exploited by current management.

10) C. A strong asset base pledged as collateral against a loan benefits lenders by increasing the likelihood of principal recovery in the event of bankruptcy (and liquidation). This, in turn, increases their willingness to provide debt to the target. The target's asset base is particularly important in the leveraged loan market, where the value of the assets helps dictate the amount of bank debt available.

11) A. A proven management team serves to increase the attractiveness (and value) of an LBO candidate. Talented management is critical in an LBO scenario given the need to operate under a highly leveraged capital structure with ambitious performance targets. Prior experience operating under such conditions, as well as success in integrating acquisitions or implementing restructuring initiatives, is highly regarded by sponsors.

12) D. Sponsor exits are realized through selling their investments to another company or sponsor and IPOs. Refinancing is a monetization but not an exit strategy for a sponsor.

13) D. Sponsors work diligently throughout the lifespan of an investment to achieve multiple expansion upon exit. There are several strategies aimed at achieving a higher exit multiple: increase in the target's size and scale (through organic growth and/or M&A), meaningful operational improvements, a repositioning of the business toward more highly valued industry segments, and the accurate timing of a cyclical sector or economic upturn.

14) D. A dividend recap provides the sponsor with the added benefit of retaining 100% of its existing ownership position in the target, thus preserving the ability to share in any future upside potential and the option to pursue a sale or IPO at a future date.

15) B. In a dividend recap, the target raises proceeds through the issuance of additional debt to pay shareholders a dividend. The incremental indebtedness may be issued in the form of an "add-on" to the target's existing credit facilities and/or bonds, a new security at the HoldCo level, or as part of a complete refinancing of the existing capital structure. The additional leverage lowers the issuer's credit strength, thereby increasing its overall risk profile.

16) A. Although IPOs do not provide sponsors with a full monetization upfront, they provide sponsors with a liquid market for its remaining equity investment while also preserving the opportunity to share in any future upside potential. Depending on equity capital market conditions, an IPO may also offer a compelling valuation premium to an outright sale.

17) C. Successful IPO execution and pricing depend on a variety of factors including equity capital markets conditions, investor sentiment, company and sector performance, and the reception to the management team on the roadshow, among other considerations.

18) B. The correct order is:

    I. First lien secured debt
    II. Senior unsecured debt
    III. Senior subordinated debt
    IV. Equity

19) D. The majority of companies utilize a revolver or equivalent lending arrangement to provide ongoing liquidity for seasonal working capital needs, capital expenditures, letters of credit, and other general corporate purposes. A revolver may also be used to fund a portion of the purchase price in an LBO, although it is usually undrawn at close. Long-term projects are typically financed with more permanent financing.

20) B. To compensate firms for offering revolving credit facilities (which may or may not be drawn upon and offers a less attractive return when unfunded), a nominal annual commitment fee is charged to the company on the undrawn

portion of the facility. The fee is assessed on an ongoing basis and accrues daily, typically at an annualized rate up to 50 basis points (bps) depending on the credit of the borrower.

21) B. The revolver is generally the least expensive form of capital in the LBO financing structure, typically priced at, or slightly below, the term loan's spread.

22) A. ABL facilities are secured by a first priority lien on all current assets (typically accounts receivable and inventory) of the borrower and may include a second priority lien on all other assets (typically PP&E).

23) B. Traditional bank lenders provide capital for revolvers and amortizing term loans, while institutional lenders provide capital for longer tenored, limited amortization term loans. Bank lenders typically consist of commercial banks, savings and loan institutions, finance companies, and the investment banks serving as arrangers.

24) A. High yield bonds afford issuers greater flexibility than bank debt due to their less restrictive incurrence covenants (and absence of maintenance covenants), longer maturities, and lack of mandatory amortization. One offsetting factor, however, is that high yield bonds have call protection/non-call features that can negatively impact a sponsor's exit strategy because PE firms are restricted from retiring debt early.

25) A. A bridge loan is a short-term loan that is used until a company is able to obtain permanent financing. They are typically outstanding for one year or less. If the bridge remains outstanding after one year, the borrower generally pays a conversion fee.

26) B. The equity contribution percentage typically ranges from approximately 25% to 40% of the LBO financing structure, although this may vary depending on debt market conditions, the type of company, and the purchase multiple paid.

27) A. Collateral represents assets, property, and/or securities pledged by a borrower to secure a loan or other debt obligation, which is subject to seizure and/or liquidation in the event of a default. It can include accounts receivable, inventory, PP&E, intellectual property, and securities such as the common stock of the borrower/issuer and its subsidiaries.

28) C. The correct order is:

    I. First lien secured debt at OpCo
    II. Second lien secured debt at OpCo
    III. Senior unsecured notes at OpCo
    IV. Senior discount notes at HoldCo

29) A. The correct order is:

    I. Revolver
    II. Term loan B
    III. Senior notes
    IV. Senior subordinated notes

Bank debt tends to have shorter maturities, often five to six years for revolvers and seven (or sometimes seven and one-half years) for institutional term loans. Historically, high yield bonds have had a maturity of seven to ten years. In an LBO financing structure comprising several debt instruments (e.g., a revolver, institutional term loans, and bonds), the revolver will mature before the institutional term loans, which, in turn, will mature before the bonds. Therefore, the correct ascending order of debt instruments is the revolver, term loan, senior notes, and senior subordinated notes.

30) C. Call premiums protect investors from having debt with an attractive yield refinanced long before maturity, thereby mitigating reinvestment risk in the event market interest rates decline. Reinvestment risk is the risk that future coupons from a bond will not be reinvested at the existing interest rate when the bond was initially purchased.

31) B. Covenants are provisions in credit agreements and indentures intended to protect against the deterioration of the borrower/issuer's credit quality. The three primary classifications of covenants are affirmative, negative, and financial.

32) D. While many of the covenants in credit agreements and indentures are similar in nature, a key difference is that traditional bank debt features financial maintenance covenants while high yield bonds have less restrictive incurrence covenants.

33) C. Financial maintenance covenants require the borrower to "maintain" a certain credit profile at all times through compliance with certain financial ratios or tests on a quarterly basis. Financial maintenance covenants are also designed to limit the borrower's ability to take certain actions that may be adverse to lenders (e.g., making capital expenditures beyond a set amount).

34) A. QIBs are institutions that, in aggregate, own and invest (on a discretionary basis) at least $100 million in securities.

35) C. Required maintenance leverage ratios typically decrease ("step down") throughout the term of a loan, while the coverage ratios typically increase over time. This requires the borrower to improve its credit profile by repaying debt and/or growing cash flow in accordance with the financial projections it presents to lenders during syndication.

36) B. The coupon rate represents the percentage of interest the purchaser of a bond will be paid by the issuer. A $1,000 bond trading at par with 6.0% interest has a coupon rate of 6.0%.

37) C. Current yield is calculated as total interest divided by the current price of the bond. 7% / $95 = 7.36%

38) A. To compensate the GP for management of the fund, LPs typically pay 1% to 2% per annum on committed funds as a management fee. In addition, once the LPs have received the return of every dollar of committed capital plus the required investment return threshold, the sponsor typically receives a 20% "carry" on every dollar of investment profit ("carried interest").

39) C. Corporations generally pay bondholders on a semiannual basis.

40) A. A shorter maturity compared to other institutional types of debt is a disadvantage. A company must pay additional fees when extending an existing revolving credit facility or entering into a new facility.

41) A. Entry and exit assumptions generally have the biggest impact on LBO valuation and the IRR. The next biggest drivers are typically the amount of debt used, followed by revenue growth.

42) C. Credit agreements govern bank debt and indentures govern bonds.

43) B. While there are few steadfast rules, certain common traits emerge among traditional LBO candidates, as outlined below.

> - Strong Cash Flow Generation
> - Leading and Defensible Market Positions
> - Growth Opportunities
> - Efficiency Enhancement Opportunities
> - Low Capex Requirements
> - Strong Asset Base
> - Proven Management Team

44) See answer below:

High yield bonds	Unsecured
Revolving credit facility	Secured
Term loan	Secured
Mezzanine debt	Unsecured
Equity	Unsecured
ABL facility	Secured

45) Debt reduction creates equity value on a dollar for dollar basis, but EBITDA is capitalized at a multiple upon exit.

46) The advantages of a sale are full exit and receipt of cash upfront. As part of this, the seller does not bear the risk of market conditions affecting a full exit through future follow-on equity offerings or an eventual sale of the company.

47) There are several strategies aimed at achieving a higher exit multiple, including an increase in the target's size and scale, meaningful operational improvements, a repositioning of the business toward more highly valued industry segments, an acceleration of the target's organic growth rate and/or profitability, and the accurate timing of a cyclical upturn, among others.

48) Examples include senior secured debt-to-EBITDA, total debt-to-EBITDA, and EBITDA-to-interest expense

49) Contractual seniority refers to the priority status of debt instruments at the same legal entity within a company.

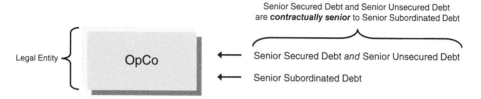

50) Structural subordination refers to the priority status of debt instruments at different legal entities within a company.

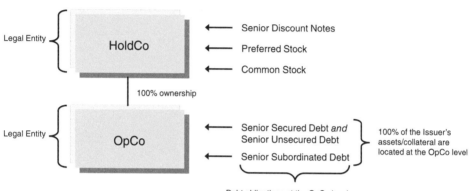

CHAPTER 5

LBO Analysis

1) Using the assumptions below, calculate ValueCo's enterprise value and equity purchase price

   ($ in millions)

Assumptions	
LTM 9/30/2012 EBITDA	$700.0
Entry EBITDA Multiple	8.0x
Total Debt	1,500.0
Cash and Cash Equivalents	250.0

   a. Calculate enterprise value

   _____

   b. Calculate equity purchase price

   _____

2) Using the enterprise value and equity purchase price determined in the prior question, as well as the following assumptions, complete the sources and uses table and answer the following questions (round numbers to nearest decimal point)

   ($ in millions)

Assumptions	
New Revolver Size (undrawn at close)	$250.0
Senior Secured Leverage	3.1x
Total Leverage	5.2x
Equity Contribution	35.0%
Cash on Hand	250.0
Tender / Call Premiums*	20.0
Financing Fees	90.0
Other Fees and Expenses	40.0
*Assume ValueCo's debt is fully refinanced	

($ in millions)

Sources of Funds			Uses of Funds	
Revolving Credit Facility	A)		Purchase ValueCo Equity	
Term Loan B	B)		Repay Existing Debt	
Senior Notes	C)		Tender / Call Premiums	
Equity Contribution	D)		Financing Fees	
Cash on Hand			Other Fees and Expenses	
Total Sources	E)		**Total Uses**	

a. Determine ValueCo's pro forma revolver balance

b. Calculate the term loan B principal amount

c. Calculate the senior notes principal amount

d. Calculate the sponsor's equity contribution

e. Determine the total sources amount

3) Given the sources & uses of funds determined in the prior question, as well as the opening balance sheet below, complete the pro forma balance sheet at closing and answer the related questions (showing all adjustments)

($ in millions)

Balance Sheet				
	Opening 2012	Adjustments +	-	Pro Forma 2012
Cash and Cash Equivalents	$250.0			
Accounts Receivable	450.0			
Inventories	600.0			
Prepaids and Other Current Assets	175.0			
Total Current Assets	**$1,475.0**			**A)**
Property, Plant and Equipment, net	2,500.0			
Goodwill	1,000.0			**B)**
Intangible Assets	875.0			
Other Assets	150.0			
Deferred Financing Fees	-			
Total Assets	**$6,000.0**			**C)**
Accounts Payable	215.0			
Accrued Liabilities	275.0			
Other Current Liabilities	100.0			
Total Current Liabilities	**$590.0**			
Revolving Credit Facility	-			
Term Loan A	-			
Term Loan B	-			
Term Loan C	-			
Existing Term Loan	1,000.0			
2nd Lien	-			
Senior Notes	-			
Existing Senior Notes	500.0			
Senior Subordinated Notes	-			
Other Debt	-			
Deferred Income Taxes	300.0			
Other Long-Term Liabilities	110.0			
Total Liabilities	**$2,500.0**			**D)**
Noncontrolling Interest	-			
Shareholders' Equity	3,500.0			
Total Shareholders' Equity	**$3,500.0**			
Total Liabilities and Equity	**$6,000.0**			**E)**

Balance Check	*0.000*	*0.000*

a. Calculate ValueCo's pro forma current assets balance

_____

b. Calculate pro forma goodwill

_____

c. Calculate pro forma total assets

_____

d. Calculate pro forma total liabilities

_____

e. Calculate pro forma shareholders' equity

_____

4) Using the LBO financing structure previously determined, as well as the assumptions below, calculate ValueCo's pro forma interest expense and appropriate coverage and leverage ratios at transaction closing

($ in millions)

Assumptions	
Revolver Pricing	L+425 bps / 1.25% LIBOR Floor
Commitment Fee on Unused Portion	50 bps
Administrative Agent Fee	$150K
Term Loan B Pricing	L+450 bps / 1.25% LIBOR Floor
Senior Notes Coupon	8.5%
2012E Capex	155.3
Financing Fee Amortization	8 years

($ in millions)

Credit Statistics	
LTM 9/30/2012 EBITDA	$700.0
Interest Expense	A)
Capex	155.3
EBITDA / Interest Expense	B)
(EBITDA - Capex) / Interest Expense	C)
Senior Secured Debt / EBITDA	D)
Total Debt / EBITDA	E)

a. Calculate ValueCo's pro forma Year 1 interest expense

_____

b. Calculate EBITDA-to-interest expense ratio

_____

c. Calculate capex-adjusted coverage ratio

_____

d. Calculate senior secured leverage ratio

_____

e. Calculate total leverage ratio

_____

5) Using previous questions, the balance sheet data below and assuming 1% per annum repayment on Term Loan B, complete ValueCo's Year 1 cash flow statement (assume all cash flow is used to repay debt) and answer the related questions

($ in millions)

Balance Sheet Data		
	2012	**2013**
Current Assets		
Accounts Receivable	450.0	483.8
Inventories	600.0	645.0
Prepaids and Other Current Assets	175.0	188.1
Current Liabilities		
Accounts Payable	215.0	231.1
Accrued Liabilities	275.0	295.6
Other Current Liabilities	100.0	107.5

Cash Flow Statement	
	2013
Operating Activities	
Net Income	$184.9
Plus: Depreciation	166.9
Plus: Amortization	55.6
Plus: Amortization of Financing Fees	12.0
Changes in Working Capital Items	
(Inc.) / Dec. in Accounts Receivable	**A)**
(Inc.) / Dec. in Inventories	
(Inc.) / Dec. in Prepaid and Other Current Assets	
Inc. / (Dec.) in Accounts Payable	**B)**
Inc. / (Dec.) in Accrued Liabilities	
Inc. / (Dec.) in Other Current Liabilities	
(Inc.) / Dec. in Net Working Capital	
Cash Flow from Operating Activities	**C)**
Investing Activities	
Capital Expenditures	(166.9)
Cash Flow from Investing Activities	**($166.9)**
Financing Activities	
Term Loan B	**D)**
Cash Flow from Financing Activities	
Excess Cash for the Period	**E)**
Beginning Cash Balance	
Ending Cash Balance	

a. Calculate ValueCo's y/y change in accounts receivable; is the amount a source or use of cash?

_____

b. Calculate ValueCo's y/y change in accounts receivable; is the amount a source or use of cash?

_____

c. Calculate 2013 cash flow from operating activities

_____

d. Calculate 2013 term loan B repayment amount

_____

e. Determine excess cash for the period, if any

_____

6) Assuming the sponsor sells ValueCo at the end of 2017 at an exit multiple
    equal to its entry multiple, determine enterprise value and equity value at exit
    given the ending debt balances provided

($ in millions)

Calculation of Exit Enterprise Value and Equity Value	
	Year 5 **2017**
2017E EBITDA	$929.2
Exit EBITDA Multiple	A)
Enterprise Value at Exit	B)
Less: Net Debt	-
Revolving Credit Facility	-
Term Loan B	763.9
Senior Notes	1,500.0
Total Debt	
Less: Cash and Cash Equivalents	-
Net Debt	C)
Equity Value at Exit	D)

a. What is the appropriate EBITDA multiple to apply to ValueCo's 2017E
    EBITDA?

b. Calculate enterprise value at exit

c. Calculate net debt

d. Calculate equity value at exit

7) Given the assumptions provided in prior questions, as well as the calculations performed, determine the IRR and cash return on the sponsor's equity contribution assuming a 2017 (Year 5) exit

($ in millions)

	Pro forma 2012	Year 1 2013	Year 2 2014	Year 3 2015	Year 4 2016	Year 5 2017
Initial Equity Investment	A)					
Equity Value at Exit					-	-
Total	-	-	-	-	-	B)
IRR	C)					
Cash Return	D)					

   a. What is the sponsor's initial equity investment?

   b. Calculate total equity value at exit

   c. Calculate IRR

   d. Calculate cash return

8) All of the following industries have traditionally supported high leverage levels EXCEPT

   A. Technology
   B. Cable
   C. Industrials
   D. Gaming

9) If a PE firm contributes $400 million of equity to a company upfront and exits the investment at the end of year five for $1,000 million, what is the internal rate of return?

   A. 19.5%
   B. 20.1%
   C. 25.7%
   D. 26.7%

10) If a PE firm contributes $225 million of equity to a company upfront and exits the investment at the end of year five for $820 million, what is the cash return?

   A. 2.5x
   B. 3.5x
   C. 3.6x
   D. 4.0x

11) Using the information below, determine the size of the term loan B and calculate the source and use of funds, respectively

($ in millions)

Sources of Funds		Uses of Funds	
Term Loan B		Purchase ValueCo Equity	$825.0
Senior Subordinated Notes	300.0	Repay Existing Debt	300.0
Equity Contribution	385.0	Financing Fees	20.0
Cash on Hand	25.0	Other Fees and Expenses	15.0
Total Sources		**Total Uses**	

   A. $300.0 million; $1,000.0 million
   B. $320.0 million; $1,425.0 million
   C. $450.0 million; $1,160.0 million
   D. Cannot be determined

Use the information below to answer the next three questions

($ in millions)

Financial Data					
	2012	**2013**	**2014**	**2015**	**2016**
Total Debt	$4,000.0	$3,500.0	$3,000.0	$2,500.0	$2,000.0
Interest Expense	600.0	465.0	400.0	330.0	240.0
EBITDA	730.0	775.0	805.0	850.0	900.0

12) Calculate the company's 2016 interest converge ratio? What does this indicate?

    A. 3.4x, stronger credit profile than 2012
    B. 3.4x, weaker credit profile than 2012
    C. 3.8x, stronger credit profile than 2012
    D. 8.3x, weaker credit profile than 2012

13) Between 2012 and 2016, total leverage _____.

    A. Decreases
    B. Increases
    C. Remains constant
    D. Cannot be determined

14) Between 2012 and 2016, the credit profile of the company _____.

    A. Weaknesses
    B. Strengthens
    C. Remains constant
    D. Cannot be determined

15) Which of the following is a reasonable total leverage ratio for an LBO under normal market conditions?

    A. 3.0x EBITDA
    B. 5.0x EBITDA
    C. 5.0x net income
    D. 1.0x sales

16) The projection period of an LBO model for a potential debt provider is typically how many years?

    A. 1-2 years
    B. 3-4 years
    C. 7-10 years
    D. 15 years+

17) Who chooses the preferred financing structure for a given LBO?

    A. Target company CEO
    B. Sponsor
    C. Investment Bank
    D. Shareholders

18) What IRR threshold has historically served as the standard for sponsors in considering an LBO?

    A. 5%
    B. 10%
    C. 20%
    D. 40%

19) Which of the following is NOT a key component of an LBO analysis transaction summary page?

    A. Sources and uses of funds
    B. Credit statistics
    C. Returns analysis
    D. Debt schedule

20) Under what circumstances might a strategic buyer use LBO analysis?

    A. To determine the debt capacity of their company
    B. To determine the price a financial sponsor bidder can afford to pay when competing for an asset in an auction process
    C. To help spread comparable companies analysis
    D. Strategic buyers would not use LBO analysis

21) What are the key variables for sensitivity analysis performed in LBO analysis?

    I. Purchase price
    II. Financing structure
    III. Historical dividends
    IV. Exit multiple

    A. I and II
    B. II and III
    C. I, II, and IV
    D. I, II, III, and IV

22) In an organized M&A sale process, what is typically the primary source for the Management Case financial projections used in the LBO model?

    A. Comparable companies analysis
    B. Research estimates
    C. Third party news providers
    D. CIM

23) Which of the following historical financial data is the least relevant for framing projections and performing LBO analysis?

    A. Sales growth
    B. EBITDA and EBIT margins
    C. Capex
    D. Interest expense

24) Which of the following is NOT a typical operating case used in LBO analysis?

    A. SEC case
    B. Base case
    C. Downside case
    D. Sponsor case

25) Which of the following is NOT a standard section of a cash flow statement?

    A. Operating activities
    B. Financing activities
    C. Investing activities
    D. Acquisition activities

26) How is goodwill created?

A. Per share premium paid for a company
B. Synergies created in a M&A transaction
C. Excess amount paid for a target over its net identifiable assets
D. Write-down on a company's balance sheet

27) Calculate goodwill if a company has $700 million of net identifiable assets and is purchased for $825 million

A. $125.0 million
B. $700.0 million
C. $1,525.0 million
D. Cannot be determined

28) Which of the following is not one of the primary GAAP financial statements?

A. Debt schedule
B. Income statement
C. Balance sheet
D. Cash flow statement

29) In an LBO analysis, which of the following are typical adjustments made to the opening balance sheet?

I. Subtraction of new LBO debt
II. Subtraction of existing shareholders' equity
III. Addition of deferred financing fees
IV. Addition of goodwill created

A. I and II
B. II and III
C. I, II, and IV
D. II, III, and IV

30) How are capex projections typically crafted?

A. Sourced from the CIM
B. Comparable companies analysis
C. Detailed inventory inspection
D. Third party news providers

31) Why are capex projections important to evaluate in an LBO analysis?

    A. Helps potential buyers evaluate their investment time horizon
    B. Capex represents a use of cash and decreases free cash flow
    C. Buyers prefer companies with large amounts of maintenance capex
    D. Buyers prefer companies with large amounts of growth capex

32) Annual deferred financing fees are

    A. Found only in LBO transactions
    B. Excluded from the post-LBO model
    C. Only used for term loan debt instruments
    D. Non-cash expenses

33) Using the information below, calculate the annual financing fees

($ in millions)

Assumptions		
	Size	Fees (%)
Term Loan B	$500.0	1.75%
Senior Notes	300.0	2.25%

    A. $12.5 million
    B. $13.5 million
    C. $14.5 million
    D. $15.5 million

34) Why is a forward LIBOR curve needed to craft the debt schedule?

    A. Deferred financing fees are dependent on LIBOR
    B. Cash flow from investing activities is dependent on LIBOR
    C. Serves as the basis for calculating interest expense for term loans
    D. Serves as the basis for calculating interest expense for senior notes

35) What is a cash flow sweep in an LBO model?

    A. All cash generated by the target after making mandatory debt repayments is applied to the optional repayment of outstanding prepayable debt

    B. All cash generated by the target after making mandatory debt repayments is used to pay dividends

    C. Three financial statements linking together

    D. A sponsor using more equity than debt for a transaction

36) What is the average interest expense convention?

    A. Methodology to use a weighted average interest expense calculation across all tranches of debt

    B. Methodology to calculate interest that must be used if a mid-year convention is also being utilized

    C. Methodology to calculate interest that takes into account the tenor of each debt instrument

    D. Methodology to calculate interest that accounts for the fact that certain debt is repaid throughout the year rather than at the beginning or end of the year

37) Which of the following is NOT a key aspect of the target's credit profile that is analyzed closely when considering a proposed transaction?

    A. Cash flow generation

    B. Ability to repay debt

    C. Pre-LBO interest payments

    D. Credit statistics

38) In LBO analysis, what assumption is usually made with regard to the exit multiple?

    A. Set equal to, or below, the entry multiple

    B. Set higher than the entry multiple

    C. Set equal to closest competitor

    D. Set higher than closest competitor

39) How does IRR typically vary with exit year?

    A. Stays constant through investment horizon

    B. Decreases due to slowing growth rates and the time value of money

    C. Increases indefinitely

    D. Increases every year until Year 5 and then decreases every year thereafter

40) Which of the following typically has the least impact on IRR?

    A. Interest rates
    B. Purchase price
    C. Projected financial performance
    D. Financing structure

41) Which of the following is not a strength of high yield bonds?

    A. Lack of maintenance covenants
    B. Lack of mandatory amortization
    C. Longer maturities
    D. Non-call features

42) How are transaction fees treated in an LBO?

    A. Amortized like financing fees
    B. Expensed as incurred
    C. Paid in stock
    D. No M&A fees in a LBO

43) How is cash flow available for debt repayment calculated?

    A. Sum of cash flow from operating activities and investing activities
    B. Sum of cash flow from investing activities and financing activities
    C. Sum of cash flow from operating activities, investing activities, and financing activities
    D. Equal to cash flow from financing activities

44) What is the typical yearly amortization fee on term loan B up until the final year bullet?

    A. 1%
    B. 3%
    C. 5%
    D. 20%

45) How does the senior notes balance change throughout a projection period in an LBO model?

    A. Decreases
    B. Decreases, but will typically be converted into equity
    C. Increases
    D. Stays constant

46) How is a PIK treated in a LBO?

    A. Treated as cash interest expense
    B. Treated as cash interest expense, but not included in average interest expense convention if that methodology is being used
    C. Treated as non-cash interest expense and added back to cash flow from operating activities on the cash flow statement
    D. Added back to cash flow from financing activities on the cash flow statement

48) What are the primary functions of LBO analysis?

_____

_____

_____

_____

49) How is LBO analysis used to analyze and craft financing structure?

_____

_____

_____

_____

50) How is LBO analysis used to determine valuation?

_____

_____

_____

_____

51) Why is historical interest expense not meaningful when building an LBO model?

_____

_____

_____

_____

52) How is cash available for optional debt repayment calculated?

_____

_____

_____

_____

53) What are common mistakes that would cause the balance sheet not to balance?

_____

_____

_____

_____

54) How is purchase price determined for a public target? For a private target?

_____

_____

_____

_____

55) How are deferred financing fees created?

_____

_____

_____

_____

56) Why does LBO analysis typically frame the lower end of the valuation range?

_____

_____

_____

_____

57) How does the income statement link to the balance sheet and cash flow statement?

_____

_____

_____

_____

1) Calculation of enterprise value and equity purchase price

| = Entry EBITDA Multiple x LTM EBITDA |
| = 8.0x x $700.0 million |

($ in millions)

Purchase Price	
Entry EBITDA Multiple	8.0x
LTM 9/30/2012 EBITDA	700.0
Enterprise Value	**$5,600.0**
Less: Total Debt	(1,500.0)
Plus: Cash and Cash Equivalents	250.0
Equity Purchase Price	**$4,350.0**

| = Enterprise Value - Total Debt + Cash and Cash Equivalents |
| = $5,600.0 million - $1,500 million + $250.0 million |

a. $5,600.0 million. Enterprise value is calculated as the entry EBITDA multiple multiplied by LTM EBITDA. (8.0x × $700.0 million)

b. $4,350.0 million. Equity purchase price is calculated as the enterprise value less total debt plus cash and cash equivalents ($5,600.0 million - $1,500 million + $250.0 million)

2) Calculation of sources and uses

($ in millions)

Sources of Funds		Uses of Funds	
Revolving Credit Facility	-	Purchase ValueCo Equity	$4,350.0
Term Loan B	2,150.0	Repay Existing Debt	1,500.0
Senior Notes	1,500.0	Tender / Call Premiums	20.0
Equity Contribution	2,100.0	Financing Fees	90.0
Cash on Hand	250.0	Other Fees and Expenses	40.0
Total Sources	**$6,000.0**	**Total Uses**	**$6,000.0**

a. Zero. The transaction assumes no revolver draw at close.

b. $2,150.0 million. Term loan B principal amount is calculated as LTM EBITDA multiplied by senior secured leverage.

($ in millions)

Calculation of Term Loan B Principal Amount	
LTM 9/30/2012 EBITDA	$700.0
Senior Secured Leverage	3.1x
Term Loan B Principal Amount	**$2,150.0**

c. $1,500.0 million. Senior notes principal amount is calculated as LTM EBITDA multiplied by the difference between total and senior secured leverage (5.2x - 3.1x).

($ in millions)

Calculation of Senior Notes Principal Amount	
LTM 9/30/2012 EBITDA	$700.0
Incremental Leverage	2.1x
Senior Notes Principal Amount	**$1,500.0**

d. $2,100.0 million. Sponsor's equity contribution is calculated as total sources less term loan B, senior notes, and cash on hand.

($ in millions)

Calculation of Equity Contribution	
Total Sources	$6,000.0
Less: Term Loan B	(2,150.0)
Less: Senior Notes	(1,500.0)
Less: Cash on Hand	(250.0)
Equity Contribution	**$2,100.0**

e. $6,000.0 million. Total sources is calculated as the sum of term loan B, senior notes, equity contribution, and cash on hand.

($ in millions)

Calculation of Total Sources	
Term Loan B	$2,150.0
Senior Notes	1,500.0
Issuance of Common Stock	2,100.0
Cash on Hand	250.0
Total Sources	**$6,000.0**

3) Balance sheet adjustments

($ in millions)

Sources of Funds			Uses of Funds		
Revolving Credit Facility	-		Purchase ValueCo Equity	$4,350.0	E
Term Loan B	2,150.0	A	Repay Existing Debt	1,500.0	F
Senior Notes	1,500.0	B	Tender / Call Premiums	20.0	G
Equity Contribution	2,100.0	C	Financing Fees	90.0	H
Cash on Hand	250.0	D	Other Fees and Expenses	40.0	I
Total Sources	**$6,000.0**		**Total Uses**	**$6,000.0**	

Balance Sheet

	Opening 2012	Adjustments +	Adjustments -	Pro Forma 2012	
Cash and Cash Equivalents	$250.0		(250.0) D	-	
Accounts Receivable	450.0			450.0	
Inventories	600.0			600.0	
Prepaids and Other Current Assets	175.0			175.0	
Total Current Assets	**$1,475.0**			**$1,225.0**	
Property, Plant and Equipment, net	2,500.0			2,500.0	
Goodwill	1,000.0	1,850.0	(1,000.0)	1,850.0	= Equity Purchase Price
Intangible Assets	875.0			875.0	Less: Net Identifiable Assets
Other Assets	150.0			150.0	= $4,350 million - ($3,500 million - $1,000 million)
Deferred Financing Fees	-	90.0		90.0	
Total Assets	**$6,000.0** H			**$6,690.0** E	
Accounts Payable	215.0			215.0	
Accrued Liabilities	275.0			275.0	
Other Current Liabilities	100.0			100.0	
Total Current Liabilities	**$590.0**			**$590.0**	
Revolving Credit Facility	-			-	
Term Loan A	-	A		-	
Term Loan B	-	2,150.0		2,150.0	
Term Loan C	-		F	-	
Existing Term Loan	1,000.0		(1,000.0)	-	
2nd Lien	-			-	
Senior Notes	-	B	F	-	
Existing Senior Notes	500.0		(500.0)	-	
Senior Subordinated Notes	-	1,500.0		1,500.0	
Other Debt	-			-	
Deferred Income Taxes	300.0			300.0	
Other Long-Term Liabilities	110.0			110.0	
Total Liabilities	**$2,500.0**			**$4,650.0**	
Noncontrolling Interest	-			-	
Shareholders' Equity	3,500.0	2,040.0	(3,500.0)	2,040.0	ValueCo's existing equity of $3,500 million
Total Shareholders' Equity	**$3,500.0**			**$2,040.0**	is eliminated through the transaction and
Total Liabilities and Equity	**$6,000.0**			**$6,690.0**	replaced with the sponsor's equity contribution
Balance Check	*0.000*			*0.000*	

= Equity Contribution - Tender / Call Premiums - Other Fees and
Expenses
= $2,100 million - $20 million - $40 million

   C   G   I

    a. $1,225.0 million. Pro forma total current assets is calculated as the sum of cash and cash equivalents, accounts receivable, inventories, and prepaids and other current assets. ($0.0 + $450.0 million + $600.0 million + $175.0 million)

    b. $1,850.0 million. Pro forma goodwill is calculated as the opening 2012 balance plus the additions made for the transaction minus existing goodwill. The additions made for the transaction refer to the purchase of ValueCo's equity for $4,350.0 million minus net identifiable assets of $2,500.0 million, which equals $1,850.0 million. ($1,000.0 million + $1,850.0 million - $1,000.0 million)

c. $6,690.0 million. Pro forma total assets is calculated as the sum of total current assets, property, plant and equipment, goodwill, intangible assets, other assets, deferred financing fees. ($1,225.0 million + 2,500.0 million + $1,850.0 million + $875.0 million + $150.0 million + $90.0 million)

d. $4,650.0 million. Pro forma total liabilities is calculated as the sum of total current liabilities, term loan B, senior subordinated notes, deferred income taxes, and other long-term liabilities. ($590.0 + $2,150.0 million + $1,500.0 million + $300.0 million + $110.0 million)

e. $6,690.0 million. Pro forma total liabilities and shareholders' equity is calculated as total liabilities plus total shareholders' equity. ($4,650.0 million + $2,040.0 million)

4) Pro forma interest expense and credit statistics

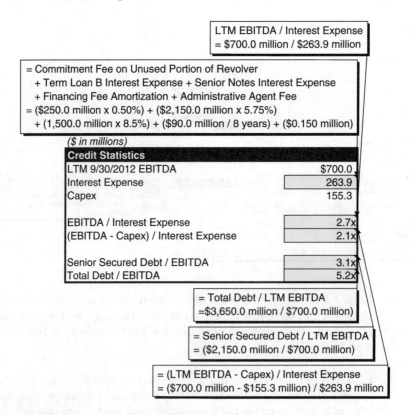

a. $263.9 million. Pro forma Year 1 interest expense is calculated as the sum of the commitment fee on the unused portion of revolver, term loan B interest expense, senior notes interest expense, financing fee amortization and the administrative agent fee. (($250.0 million × 0.50%) + ($2,150.0 million × 5.75%) + ($1,500.0 million × 8.5%) + ($90.0 million / 8 years) + ($0.150 million))

b. 2.7x. EBITDA-to-interest expense is calculated as LTM EBITDA divided by interest expense. ($700.0 million / $263.9 million)

c. 2.1x. (EBITDA-capex)-to-interest expense is calculated as LTM EBITDA less capex divided by interest expense. (($700.0 million - $155.3 million) / $263.9 million)

d. 3.1x. Senior secured debt-to-EBITDA is calculated as the total amount of senior secured debt divided by LTM EBITDA. ($2,150.0 million / $700.0 million)

e. 5.2x. Total debt-to-EBTIDA is calculated as the total amount of debt divided by LTM EBITDA. ($3,650.0 million / $700.0 million)

5) Cash flow statement

= Net Income + Depreciation + Amortization + Amortization of Financing Fees
+ (Inc.) / Dec. in Net Working Capital
= $184.9 million + $166.9 million + $55.6 million + $12.0 million - $47.6 million

= Accounts Payable$_{2013E}$ - Accounts Payable$_{2012E}$
= $231.1 million - $215.0 million

= Accounts Receivable$_{2012E}$ - Accounts Receivable$_{2013E}$
= $450.0 million - $483.8 million

($ in millions)

Cash Flow Statement	
	2013
Operating Activities	
Net Income	$184.9
Plus: Depreciation	166.9
Plus: Amortization	55.6
Plus: Amortization of Financing Fees	12.0
Changes in Working Capital Items	
(Inc.) / Dec. in Accounts Receivable	(33.8)
(Inc.) / Dec. in Inventories	(45.0)
(Inc.) / Dec. in Prepaid and Other Current Assets	(13.1)
Inc. / (Dec.) in Accounts Payable	16.1
Inc. / (Dec.) in Accrued Liabilities	20.6
Inc. / (Dec.) in Other Current Liabilities	7.5
(Inc.) / Dec. in Net Working Capital	(47.6)
Cash Flow from Operating Activities	**$371.8**
Investing Activities	
Capital Expenditures	(166.9)
Cash Flow from Investing Activities	**($166.9)**
Financing Activities	
Term Loan B	(204.9)
Cash Flow from Financing Activities	**($204.9)**
Excess Cash for the Period	-
Beginning Cash Balance	-
Ending Cash Balance	-

= Cash Flow from Operating Activities
+ Cash Flow from Investing Activities
+ Cash Flow from Financing Activities
= $371.8 million - $166.9 million - $204.9 million

= Mandatory Repayments on Term Loan B + Optional Repayments
= (2,150.0 million x 1%) + ($371.5 million - $166.9 million - $21.5 million)

a. ($33.8) million. (Inc.) / dec. in accounts receivable for 2013 is calculated as 2012 accounts receivable less 2013 accounts receivable. ($450.0 million - $483.8 million). An increase in an asset is a use of cash (represented by a negative value on the cash flow statement) and a decrease in an asset represents a source of cash

b. $16.1 million. Inc. / (dec.) in accounts payable for 2013 is calculated as 2013 accounts payable less 2012 accounts payable. ($231.1 million - $215.0 million). An increase in a liability is a source of cash and a decrease in a liability (represented by a negative value on the cash flow statement) represents a use of cash

c. $371.5 million. Cash flow from operating activities is calculated as the sum of net income, depreciation, amortization, amortization of financing fees and (inc.) / dec. in net working capital. ($184.9 million + $166.9 million + $55.6 million + $12.0 million - $47.6 million)

d. $204.6 million. Term loan B's 2013 repayment amount is calculated as mandatory repayments on term loan B plus optional repayments. ((2,150.0 million × 1%) + ($371.8 million - $166.9 million - $21.5 million))

e. Zero. Excess cash for the period is zero, calculated as the sum of cash flow from operating activities, cash flow from investing activities, and cash flow from financing activities ($371.8 million - $166.9 million - $204.9 million)

6) Enterprise value and equity value at exit

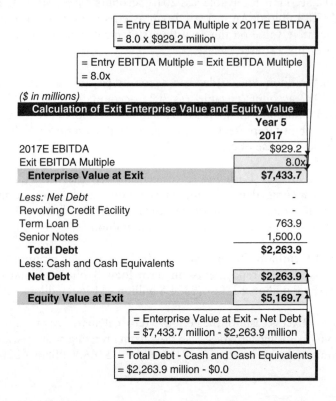

($ in millions)	
Calculation of Exit Enterprise Value and Equity Value	
	Year 5
	2017
2017E EBITDA	$929.2
Exit EBITDA Multiple	8.0x
Enterprise Value at Exit	**$7,433.7**
Less: Net Debt	-
Revolving Credit Facility	-
Term Loan B	763.9
Senior Notes	1,500.0
Total Debt	**$2,263.9**
Less: Cash and Cash Equivalents	-
Net Debt	**$2,263.9**
Equity Value at Exit	**$5,169.7**

a. 8.0x. In a traditional LBO analysis, it is common practice to conservatively assume an exit multiple equal to (or below) the entry multiple

b. $7,433.7 million. Enterprise value at exit is calculated as 2017E EBITDA multiplied by the exit EBITDA multiple. ($929.2 million × 8.0x)

c. $2,263.9 million. Net debt is calculated as total debt less cash and cash equivalents. ($2,263.9 million - $0.0)

d. $5,169.7 million. Equity value at exit is calculated as enterprise value at exit less net debt. ($7,433.7 million - $2,263.9 million)

7) IRR and cash return

($ in millions)

	Pro forma 2012	Year 1 2013	Year 2 2014	Year 3 2015	Year 4 2016	Year 5 2017
Initial Equity Investment	($2,100.0)					
Equity Value at Exit	-			-	-	5,169.7
Total	($2,100.0)	-	-	-	-	**$5,169.7**
IRR	20%					
Cash Return	2.5x					

=IRR (Initial Equity Investment : Equity Value at Exit)
=IRR (-$2,100 million : $5,169.7 million)

= Equity Value at Exit / Initial Equity Investment
= $5,169.7 million / $2,100.0 million

a. $2,100.0 million. The sponsor's initial equity investment is the equity contribution calculated in question #2.

b. $5,169.7 million. The total equity value at exit is calculated in question #6.

c. ~20%. IRR, which measures the total return on a sponsor's equity investment, is calculated as shown below:

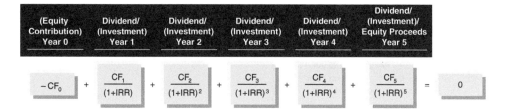

(Equity Contribution) Year 0	Dividend/ (Investment) Year 1	Dividend/ (Investment) Year 2	Dividend/ (Investment) Year 3	Dividend/ (Investment) Year 4	Dividend/ (Investment)/ Equity Proceeds Year 5

$$-CF_0 + \frac{CF_1}{(1+IRR)} + \frac{CF_2}{(1+IRR)^2} + \frac{CF_3}{(1+IRR)^3} + \frac{CF_4}{(1+IRR)^4} + \frac{CF_5}{(1+IRR)^5} = 0$$

In excel, use: IRR(Initial Equity Investment : Equity Value at Exit). (IRR (-$2,100.0 million : $5,169.7 million)

d. 2.5x. Cash return is calculated as the equity value at exit divided by the initial equity investment. ($5,169.7 million / $2,100.0 million)

8) A. For highly cyclical industries (e.g., technology), both the capital markets and rating agencies take a more conservative view towards leverage to help ensure the company is appropriately capitalized to withstand cycle troughs. On the other end of the spectrum, companies in sectors that have highly visible cash flows (e.g., cable, industrial, gaming) are typically able to maintain a more highly leveraged capital structure.

9)   B. See calculation below:

($ in millions)

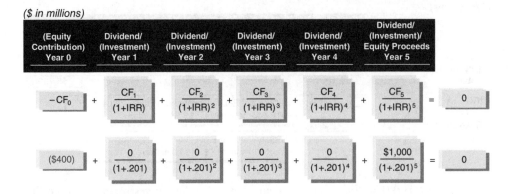

10) C. In addition to IRR, sponsors also examine returns on the basis of a multiple of their cash investment ("cash return"). However, unlike IRR, the cash return approach does not factor in the time value of money. Cash return is calculated as the equity value at exit divided by the initial equity investment.

11) C. As shown below, total sources is equal to total uses. Term loan B amount is calculated by subtracting senior subordinated notes, equity contribution and cash on hand from the total sources amount.

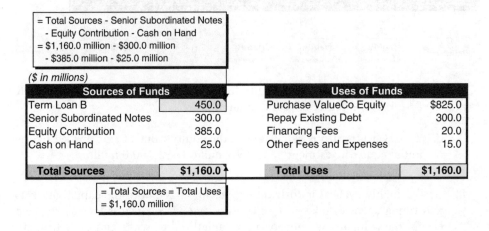

12) C. Interest coverage ratio is calculated as EBITDA divided by interest expense. Intuitively, the higher the coverage ratio, the better positioned the company is to meet its debt obligations and, therefore, the stronger its credit profile.

13) A. Total debt decreases by half over four years. As a result, the company's leverage ratio, calculated as total debt divided by EBITDA, also decreases.

14) B. The total leverage ratio decreases while interest coverage ratio increases, indicating a stronger credit profile.

15) B. The average credit statistics for LBO transactions has fluctuated dramatically over the last decade. Beginning in 2002, the total debt-to-EBITDA multiple for the average LBO was 3.9x. By 2007, this multiple reached a peak level of 6.1x, indicating extremely favorable conditions for borrowers/issuers. When credit conditions became tight in 2008 and 2009 during the credit crisis, credit statistics for LBO transactions became stronger (more favorable for lenders and debt investors and less favorable for borrowers/issuers). By 2010/2011, credit statistics reflected more normalized levels by historical standards, and averaged 4.9x total debt-to-EBITDA in 2011.

16) C. From a debt financing perspective, the projection period for an LBO model is typically set at seven to ten years so as to match the maturity of the longest tenured debt instrument in the capital structure.

17) B. Investment banks work closely with sponsor clients to determine an appropriate financing structure for a particular transaction but ultimately the sponsor chooses the preferred financing structure for an LBO (often a compilation of the best terms from proposals solicited from several banks).

18) C. While multiple factors affect a sponsor's ultimate decision to pursue a potential acquisition, comfort with meeting acceptable IRR thresholds is critical. Sponsors typically target superior returns relative to alternative investments for their LPs, with a 20%+ threshold historically serving as a widely held "rule of thumb." This threshold, however, may increase or decrease depending on market conditions, the perceived risk of an investment, and other factors specific to the situation.

19) D. An LBO analysis transaction summary provides an overview of the LBO analysis in a user-friendly format, typically displaying the sources and uses of funds, acquisition multiples, summary returns analysis, and summary financial data, as well as projected capitalization and credit statistics.

20) B. For a strategic buyer, LBO analysis (along with those derived from other valuation methodologies) is used to frame valuation and bidding strategy by analyzing the price that a competing sponsor bidder might be willing to pay for the target.

21) C. LBO valuation output is premised on key variables such as financial projections, purchase price, and financing structure, as well as exit multiple and year. Sensitivity analysis is performed on these key value drivers to produce a range of IRRs used to frame valuation for the target.

22) D. When performing LBO analysis, the first step is to collect, organize, and analyze all available information on the target, its sector, and the specifics of the transaction. In an organized sale process, the sell-side advisor provides such detail to prospective buyers, including financial projections that usually form the basis for the initial LBO model. This information is typically contained in a CIM, with additional information provided via a management presentation and data room.

23) D. When building a pre-LBO model, the historical income statement is generally only built through EBIT, as the target's prior annual interest expense and net income are not relevant given that the target will be recapitalized through the LBO.

24) A. The "Base Case" is generally premised on management assumptions, but with adjustments made based on the deal team's independent due diligence, research, and perspectives. The bank's internal credit committee(s) also requires the deal team to analyze the target's performance under one or more stress cases in order to gain comfort with the target's ability to service and repay debt during periods of duress, known as "Downside Case". The operating scenario that the deal team ultimately uses to set covenants and market the transaction to investors is provided by the sponsor ("Sponsor Case").

25) D. The cash flow statement consists of three sections—operating activities, investing activities, and financing activities.

26) C. Goodwill is created from the excess amount paid for a target over its net identifiable assets. The goodwill created remains on the balance sheet (unamortized) over the life of the investment, but is tested annually for impairment.

27) A. Goodwill is calculated as equity purchase price less net identifiable assets.

28) A. The primary financial statements are the income statement, balance sheet, and the cash flow statement.

29) D. Typical adjustments include the subtraction of existing shareholders' equity, addition of deferred financing fees, and addition of goodwill created as well as the repayment of debt and addition of tender/call premiums in some situations.

30) A. Projected capex assumptions are typically sourced from the CIM. In the event that capex projections are not provided/available, the banker typically projects capex as a fixed percentage of sales at historical levels with appropriate adjustments for cyclical or non-recurring items

31) B. Capex is typically the key line item under investing activities. The target's projected net PP&E must incorporate the capex projections (added to PP&E) as well as those for depreciation (subtracted from PP&E.) The sum of the annual cash flows provided by operating activities and investing activities provides annual cash flow available for debt repayment, which is commonly referred to as free cash flow.

32) D. The amortization of deferred financing fees is a non-cash expense that is added back to net income in the post-LBO cash flow statement.

33) D. See calculation below:

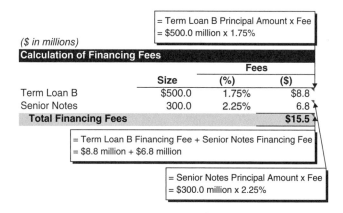

34) C. For floating-rate debt instruments, such as revolving credit facilities and term loans, interest rates are typically based on LIBOR plus a fixed spread. Therefore, to calculate their projected annual interest expense, the banker must first enter future LIBOR estimates for each year of the projection period.

35) A. A typical LBO model employs a "100% cash flow sweep" that assumes all cash generated by the target after making mandatory debt repayments is

applied to the optional repayment of outstanding prepayable debt (typically bank debt). For modeling purposes, bank debt is generally repaid in the following order: revolver balance, term loan A, term loan B, etc.

36) D. The banker typically employs an average interest expense approach in determining annual interest expense in an LBO model. This methodology accounts for the fact that bank debt is repaid throughout the year rather than at the beginning or end of the year. Annual average interest expense for each debt tranche is calculated by multiplying the average of the beginning and ending debt balances in a given year by its corresponding interest rate.

37) C. Cash flow generation and the ability to repay debt and improve credit stats (e.g., debt-to-EBITDA, EBITDA-to-interest expense) are analyzed closely before a transaction. Typically, lenders look for the bank debt to be repaid within its tenor.

38) A. The exit multiple is typically set equal to, or below, entry multiple for conservatism.

39) B. IRR typically decreases in accordance with the declining growth rates and the time value of money.

40) A. The primary IRR drivers include the target's projected financial performance, purchase price, and financing structure (particularly the size of the equity contribution), as well as the exit multiple and year. As would be expected, a sponsor seeks to minimize the price paid and equity contribution while gaining a strong degree of confidence in the target's future financial performance and the ability to exit at a sufficient valuation.

41) D. High yield bonds afford issuers greater flexibility than bank debt due to their less restrictive incurrence covenants (and absence of maintenance covenants), longer maturities, and lack of mandatory amortization. One offsetting factor, however, is that high yield bonds have non-call features that can negatively impact a sponsor's exit strategy.

42) B. Other fees and expenses typically include payments for services such as M&A advisory, legal, accounting, and consulting, as well as other miscellaneous deal-related costs. Within the context of the LBO sources and uses, this amount is netted upfront against the equity contribution.

43) A. The annual projected cash available for debt repayment is the sum of the cash flows provided by operating and investing activities on the cash flow statement. For each year in the projection period, this amount is first used to make mandatory debt repayments on the term loan tranches. The remaining cash flow is used to make optional debt repayments.

44) A. Term loan facilities are fully funded at close and have a set amortization schedule as defined in the corresponding credit agreement. While amortization schedules vary per term loan tranche, the standard for TLBs is 1% amortization per year on the principal amount of the loan with a bullet payment of the loan balance at maturity.

45) D. Unlike traditional bank debt, high yield bonds are not prepayable without penalty and do not have a mandatory repayment schedule prior to the bullet payment at maturity. As a result, LBO models do not assume repayment of the high yield bonds prior to maturity and the beginning and ending balances for each year in the projection period are equal.

46) C. During robust credit markets, companies have been able to issue bonds with atypical "issuer-friendly" provisions, such as a payment-in-kind (PIK) toggle. The PIK toggle allows an issuer to choose whether to pay interest "in-kind" (i.e., in the form of additional notes) or in cash. In a capital structure with a PIK instrument, the non-cash interest portion is included in total interest expense and added back to cash flow from operating activities on the cash flow statement.

48) It is used as a core analytical tool to assess financing structure, investment returns, and valuation in leveraged buyout scenarios.

49) LBO analysis enables the banker to analyze a given financing structure on the basis of cash flow generation, debt repayment, credit statistics, and investment returns over a projection period and under multiple operating scenarios.

50) LBO analysis is also an essential component of an M&A toolset. It is used by sponsors, bankers, and other finance professionals to determine an implied valuation range for a given target in a potential LBO sale based on achieving acceptable returns. Valuation output is premised on assumptions for financial projections, purchase/exit price, and financing structure.

51)   The target's prior annual interest expense and net income are not relevant given that the target will be recapitalized with a new capital structure and associated debt terms through the LBO.

52)   The annual projected cash available for debt repayment is the sum of the cash flows provided by operating and investing activities on the cash flow statement. For each year in the projection period, this amount is first used to make mandatory debt repayments on the term loan tranches. The remaining cash flow is used to make optional debt repayments.

53)   Common missteps include depreciation or capex not being properly linked to PP&E and/or changes in balance sheet accounts not being properly reflected in the cash flow statement.

54)   For a public company, the equity purchase price is calculated by multiplying the offer price per share by the target's fully diluted shares outstanding. Net debt is then added to the equity purchase price to arrive at an implied enterprise value. For a private company, the enterprise value is calculated as LTM EBITDA multiplied by a purchase multiple.

55)   Fees for each debt tranche are multiplied by the committed amount. Annual deferred financing fees for each tranche are then determined by dividing the overall fees by the debt tranche's maturity (years).

56)   It frames the lower end of the range due to the constraints imposed by an LBO, including leverage capacity, credit market conditions, and the sponsor's own IRR hurdles. Furthermore, strategic buyers are typically able to realize synergies from the target, thereby enhancing their ability to earn a targeted return on their invested capital at a higher purchase price.

57)   Net income for each year in the projection period is linked from the income statement to the cash flow statement as the first line item under operating activities. It also feeds into the balance sheet as an addition to shareholders' equity in the form of retained earnings.

CHAPTER 6

Sell-Side M&A

1) Which one of the following is NOT a potential weakness of an auction process?

    A. Information leakage
    B. Collusion among bidders
    C. Employee morale might be negatively affected
    D. Likelihood of leaving "money on the table"

2) The advantages of a broad auction include

    I. Limiting buyers negotiating leverage
    II. Preserves likelihood of confidentially
    III. Ability to approach all possible buyers
    IV. Gives Board of Directors confidence it fulfilled its fiduciary duties

    A. II and IV
    B. I, III, and IV
    C. II, III, and IV
    D. I, II, III, and IV

3) The potential disadvantages of a targeted auction include all of the following EXCEPT

    A. Potential to exclude certain buyers
    B. Greatest risk of business disruption
    C. Not maximizing competitive dynamics
    D. Buyers have more leverage

4) Which of the following is the LEAST important criterion when evaluating strategic buyers?

    A. M&A track record of buyer
    B. LBO financing package
    C. Cultural fit
    D. Strategic fit

5) Which of the following is LEAST relevant when evaluating potential sponsor buyers?

   A. Number of partners at fund
   B. Fund size
   C. Investment strategy
   D. Sector focus

6) Which of the following are the two main marketing documents for the first round of an auction process?

   A. Teaser & confidentiality agreement
   B. Teaser & confidential information memorandum
   C. Teaser & bid procedures letter
   D. Bid procedures letter & confidentiality agreement

7) Which of the following is not included in a typical teaser?

   A. Company overview
   B. Detailed financial section with MD&A
   C. Investment highlights
   D. Contact information of sell-side bankers

8) Which entity might cause sell-side investment bankers to create a modified version of the CIM?

   A. Buyer who is public
   B. Buyer who is a competitor
   C. Financial sponsors
   D. International buyers

9) Are potential acquisition candidates included in a CIM?

   A. Yes, occasionally
   B. Yes, in a modified version of the CIM for strategic buyers only
   C. Always
   D. Never

10) Which of the following are typically included by buyers when they submit a bid during first round of M&A negotiations?

   I. Assumptions to arrive at purchase price
   II. Purchase price
   III. Future role of target management and employees
   IV. Key conditions for signing and closing

   A. II and III
   B. I, II, and IV
   C. II, III, and IV
   D. I, II, III, and IV

11) Stapled financing refers to

   A. Bidder evidence of committed financing
   B. Pre-packaged financing structure often offered by the sell-side investment bank
   C. Using only term loans in the financing structure
   D. Using only fixed interest debt instruments

12) All of the following are included in a final bid procedure letter, EXCEPT

   A. Evidence of committed financing
   B. Purchase price presented as a range
   C. Required regulatory approvals
   D. Confirmation that the offer is binding

13) A material adverse change

   A. Allows competitive bidders to re-enter the process
   B. Could permit a buyer to avoid closing a transaction
   C. Allows the government to block a transaction
   D. Mandates regulators to block a transition

14) Who is typically hired to render a fairness opinion?

    I. Investment banking firm serving as sell-side advisor
    II. Investment banking firm not serving as sell-side advisor
    III. Corporate law firm serving as sell-side advisor legal counsel
    IV. Consulting firm working with the selling company

    A. I and II
    B. I and IV
    C. II and III
    D. III and IV

15) Which of the following laws is critical for closing an M&A deal?

    A. Glass-Steagall Act of 1933
    B. Hart-Scott-Rodino Antitrust Improvements Act Of 1976
    C. Gramm-Leach–Bliley Act of 1999
    D. Sarbanes-Oxley Act of 2002

16) If more than _____ of an acquirer's pre-deal common shares outstanding are being offered as a form of consideration in a transaction, the acquirer needs to obtain shareholder approval.

    A. 10%
    B. 15%
    C. 20%
    D. 25%

17) In a two-step merger process, what percentage of tendered shares does the acquirer generally need to reach to execute a squeeze-out scenario?

    A. 50%
    B. 60%
    C. 70%
    D. 90%

18) If an acquirer needs access to the capital markets for a deal, when does the marketing process for the financing typically begin?

    A. Before the first round
    B. Before the end of the second round
    C. After the second round
    D. After signing of the definitive agreement

19) Which of the following is NOT an advantage of a negotiated sale?

A. Minimizes potential of "taint" perception
B. Generally fastest time to signing
C. Highest degree of confidentiality
D. Ensures all potential bidders are contacted

20) Negotiated sales are often initiated by

A. Customers
B. Buyers
C. Regulators
D. Corporate law firms

21) Which of the following is NOT a sufficient reason for shareholders to endorse one company acquiring another company?

A. Target is undervalued
B. Gain market share
C. CEO wants to manage a larger company
D. Target has critical assets the buyer wants/needs

22) Which of the following describes a "no-shop" provision?

A. Used by senior executives to prevent a company from being put up for sale
B. Used by boards to prevent a company from being put up for sale
C. Prevents sponsors from shopping around for other companies for a specific period of time once they sign a definitive agreement to purchase a company
D. Measure to prevent seller from soliciting third party offers after a merger agreement has been signed

23) A break-up fee typically falls within what percentage of the offer value?

A. 1%-5%
B. 5%-10%
C. 10%-15%
D. 15%-20%

24) When drafting a CIM, which of the following parties typically interacts the least with the sell-side investment bank?

   A. Client CEO
   B. Client CFO
   C. Client Division Heads
   D. Client Investor Relations Head

25) How long does a typical auction take?

   A. 3-6 months
   B. 4-6 weeks
   C. 24 months
   D. 20 days

26) How long are buyers generally given to assess the target and submit a first round bid?

   A. 4-6 months
   B. 4-6 weeks
   C. 24 months
   D. 20 days

27) Select ALL that apply. Which of the following marketing documents contains detailed financial projections?

   I. Final bid procedures letter
   II. CIM
   III. Management presentation
   IV. Teaser

   A. I and II
   B. II and III
   C. II and IV
   D. I, III, and IV

28) Select ALL that apply. Which of the following are key provisions of a confidentiality agreement?

   I. Use of information
   II. Term
   III. Permitted disclosures
   IV. Non-solicitation/no hire

   A. I and IV
   B. II and III
   C. II and IV
   D. I, II, III, and IV

29) What document outlines the details and process for submitting first round bids?

   A. Final bid procedures letter
   B. Teaser
   C. Initial bid procedures letter
   D. Confidentiality agreement

30) What is the key legal document establishing a formal agreement between a buyer and seller to purchase the target?

   A. Confidentiality agreement
   B. Indenture
   C. Definitive purchase/sale agreement
   D. Credit agreement

31) What event usually marks the launch of a typical auction process?

   A. Receipt of the CIM and management projections
   B. Management presentation and access to the data room
   C. Buyer contact and distribution of the teaser
   D. Receipt of final bids from prospective buyers

32) What event typically marks the launch of the second round?

   A. Receipt of final bids from prospective buyers
   B. Management presentation and access to the data room
   C. Receipt of the CIM and management projections
   D. Buyer contact and distribution of the teaser

33) Select ALL that apply. Which of the following are key provisions of a definitive agreement?

    I. Representations and warranties
    II. Closing conditions
    III. Historical financial overview
    IV. Summary of operations

    A. I and II
    B. I and III
    C. III and IV
    D. I, II, III, and IV

34) An M&A transaction involving a public target where its shareholders vote on whether to approve or reject the proposed transaction at a formal shareholders' meeting is commonly referred to as a _____ merger

    A. 338(h)(10)
    B. Two-step
    C. One-step
    D. Asset deal

35) An M&A transaction involving a public target where a tender offer is made directly to the target's shareholders with the target's approval pursuant to a definitive agreement, with any untendered shares to be "squeezed out" if a certain threshold is met, is commonly referred to as a _____ merger.

    A. One-step
    B. Asset deal
    C. 338(h)(10)
    D. Two-step

36) Under the most favorable scenario, approximately how long can a two-step process take?

    A. 10 days
    B. 2 weeks
    C. 5-6 weeks
    D. 6 months

37) Provide two pros and two cons of running a broad auction

Pros:

    i. _____

    ii. _____

Cons:

    iii. _____

    iv. _____

38) Under what circumstances might a targeted auction be more appropriate than a broad auction?

_____

_____

_____

_____

39) Why do companies typically hire an M&A sell-side advisor?

_____

_____

_____

_____

40) Under what circumstances might the sell-side advisor recommend a negotiated sale?

_____

_____

_____

_____

41) How many parties are typically contacted in a targeted auction? Broad auction?

Targeted auction: _____

Broad auction: _____

42) List the key stages of an auction process in order from start to finish

- _____

- _____

- _____

- _____

- _____

43) What do the first round and second round of an auction process refer to?

First round: _____

_____

_____

Second round: _____

_____

_____

44) Why are the target's financial projections in an M&A sale process so important?

_____

_____

_____

_____

45) What is a teaser, and what general items does it contain?

_____

_____

_____

_____

46) When is the teaser distributed to prospective buyers?

_____

_____

_____

_____

47) At what stage is the CIM distributed? What is the key gating item for the seller prior to distribution?

_____

_____

_____

_____

48) What is the primary function of the data room and what are its general components?

_____

_____

_____

_____

49) What is the purpose of the management presentation and who typically presents?

_____

_____

_____

_____

50) What is buyer due diligence? What are the typical forms through which a buyer can conduct due diligence during a sale process?

_____

_____

_____

_____

1) D. An auction is a staged process whereby a target is marketed to multiple prospective buyers. Potential drawbacks of an auction include information leakage into the market from bidders, negative impact on employee morale, possible collusion among bidders, reduced negotiating leverage once a "winner" is chosen (thereby encouraging re-trading), and "taint" in the event of a failed auction.

2) B. Preserving confidentially is not an advantage of a broad auction. In a broad auction, the target is marketed to numerous strategic and financial buyers to maximize value, which typically results in information leakage. Heightening competitive dynamics and thus enhancing the probability of achieving a maximum sale price is the ultimate goal of an auction process.

3) B. The greatest risk of business disruption applies to a broad auction. Other disadvantages of a targeted auction include potentially leaving "money on the table" and providing Board of Directors with less market data they can use to make certain they achieved maximum value.

4) B. When evaluating strategic buyers, the banker looks first and foremost at strategic fit, including potential synergies. Financial capacity or "ability to pay"—which is typically dependent on size, balance sheet strength, access to financing, and risk appetite—is also closely scrutinized. Other factors play a role in assessing potential strategic bidders, such as cultural fit, M&A track record, existing management's role going forward, relative and pro forma market position (including antitrust concerns), and effects on existing customer and supplier relationships. LBO financing, on the other hand, is critical for a financial sponsor buyer.

5) A. When evaluating potential financial sponsor buyers, key criteria include investment strategy/focus, sector expertise, fund size, track record, fit within existing investment portfolio, fund life cycle, and ability to obtain financing. As part of this process, the deal team looks for sponsors with existing portfolio companies that may serve as an attractive combination candidate for the target.

6) B. The two main marketing documents for the first round are the teaser and the CIM. The teaser, a brief 1-2 page synopsis of the target, is the first marketing document presented to prospective buyers. The CIM is a detailed written description of the target (often 50+ pages) that serves as the primary marketing document for the target in an auction.

7) B. The teaser, which is sent upon signing of the CA, does not contain a detailed financial section with MD&A. The CIM, however, contains an in-depth financial section with a narrative by management explaining past and future performance.

8) B. A modified version of the CIM may be prepared for designated strategic buyers, namely competitors with whom the seller may be concerned about sharing certain sensitive information.

9) A. In some cases, the CIM provides additional financial information to help guide both strategic and financial buyers toward potential growth/acquisition scenarios for the target. For example, the sell-side advisor may work with management to compile a list of potential acquisition opportunities for inclusion in the CIM (typically on an anonymous basis), including their incremental sales and EBITDA contributions.

10) D. All of the answer choices are typically included when buyers submit a bid during first round of M&A negotiations. In addition, the bid may include structural considerations, information on financing sources, required approvals, and timing parameters.

11) B. Stapled financing is when the investment bank running an auction process (or a designated third party bank) offers a pre-packaged financing structure, typically for prospective financial buyers, in support of the target being sold. While buyers are not obligated to use the staple, it is designed to send a strong signal of support from the sell-side bank and provide comfort that the necessary financing will be available to buyers for the acquisition.

12) B. While presenting the purchase price as a range is common on an initial bid procedure letter, on a final bid procedure letter the purchase price must be presented as an exact amount. Other elements of a final bid procedure letter include a markup of the draft definitive agreement, attestation to completion of due diligence, and board of directors approvals.

13) B. A material adverse charge (MAC), or material adverse effects (MAE), is a highly negotiated provision in the definitive agreement, which may permit a buyer to avoid closing the transaction in the event that a substantial adverse situation is discovered after signing or a detrimental post-signing event occurs that affects the target.

14) A. Historically, the investment bank serving as sell-side advisor to the target has typically rendered the fairness opinion. In recent years, however, the ability of

the sell-side advisor to objectively evaluate the target has come under increased scrutiny. This line of thinking presumes that the sell-side advisor has an inherent bias toward consummating a transaction when a significant portion of the advisor's fee is based on the closing of the deal and/or if a stapled financing is provided by the advisor's firm to the winning bidder.

15) B. The primary regulatory approval requirement for the majority of U.S. M&A transactions is made in accordance with the Hart-Scott-Rodino Antitrust Improvements Act of 1976 (the "HSR Act"). Depending on the size of the transaction, the HSR Act requires both parties to an M&A transaction to file respective notifications and report forms with the Federal Trade Commission (FTC) and Antitrust Division of the Department of Justice (DOJ).

16) C. 20% of pre-deal common shares being offered in a deal is the threshold that requires the acquirer to get shareholder approval.

17) D. A public acquisition can be structured as a "two-step" tender offer on either a negotiated or unsolicited basis, followed by a merger. In Step I of the two-step process, the tender offer is made directly to the target's public shareholders with the target's approval pursuant to a definitive agreement. If the requisite threshold of tendered shares is reached as designed (typically 90%), the acquirer can subsequently consummate a back-end "short form" merger (Step II) to squeeze out.

18) D. The acquirer begins the marketing process for the financing following the signing of the definitive agreement so as to be ready to fund expeditiously once all of the conditions to closing are met.

19) D. A negotiated sale is between the target and one buyer, so not all potential bidders are contacted. Other advantages of a negotiated sale include: less business disruption to the target and it may be the only basis on which a credible buyer will participate in a sale process.

20) B. A negotiated sale is often initiated by a buyer, whether as the culmination of months or years of research, direct discussion between buyer and seller executives, or as a move to preempt an auction ("preemptive bid").

21) C. The fact that a CEO of a company wants to manage a larger company is not a sufficient reason to acquire another company. Key drivers for two companies

to merge are to obtain strategic assets, new geographies, new products, new customers, and synergies, among others.

22) D. A "no-shop" provision is an agreement between a seller and a buyer that prohibits the seller from soliciting a purchase proposal from any other party. This prevents the seller from soliciting other bids that may be higher than the original buyer's bid.

23) A. Break-ups fees generally fall within 1%-5% of the offer value. A typical break-up fee is paid to the previous contracted buyer in the event the seller accepts a higher offer from another party.

24) D. The deal team spends a great deal of time (typically several weeks) working with the target's CEO, CFO, and division heads to draft the CIM which is sent to potential buyers.

25) A. The traditional auction is structured as a two-round bidding process that generally spans from three to six months from the decision to sell until the signing of a definitive purchase/sale agreement ("definitive agreement") with the winning bidder. The timing of the post-signing ("closing") period depends on a variety of factors not specific to an auction, such as regulatory approvals and/or third-party consents, financing, and shareholder approval.

26) B. Prospective buyers are typically afforded 4-6 weeks to evaluate the target and submit a first round bid.

27) B. The CIM contains a detailed financial section presenting historical and projected financial information with accompanying narrative explaining both past and expected future performance (MD&A). This data forms the basis for the preliminary valuation analysis performed by prospective buyers. The management presentation is typically structured as a slideshow with accompanying hardcopy handout. The presentation format generally maps to that of the CIM, but is more crisp and concise.

28) D. The key provisions of a confidentiality agreement also include return of confidential information, standstill agreement, and restriction on clubbing.

29) C. The initial bid procedures letter, which is typically sent out to prospective buyers following distribution of the CIM, states the date and time by which

interested parties must submit their written, non-binding preliminary indications of interest ("first round bids"). It also defines the exact information that should be included in the bid.

30) C. The definitive agreement is a legally binding contract between a buyer and seller detailing the terms and conditions of the sale transaction. Definitive agreements involving public and private companies differ in terms of content, although the basic format of the document is the same, containing an overview of the transaction structure/deal mechanics, representations and warranties, pre-closing commitments (including covenants), closing conditions, termination provisions, and indemnities (if applicable), as well as associated disclosure schedules and exhibits.

31) C. The first round begins with the contacting of prospective buyers, which marks the formal launch of the auction process. This typically takes the form of a scripted phone call to each prospective buyer by a senior member of the sell-side advisory deal team (either an M&A banker or the coverage banker that maintains the relationship with the particular buyer).

32) B. The second round of the auction centers on facilitating the prospective buyers' ability to conduct detailed due diligence and analysis so they can submit strong, final (and ideally) binding bids by the set due date. The management presentation typically marks the formal kickoff of the second round, often spanning a full business day. In conjunction with the management presentation and site visits, prospective buyers are provided access to the data room.

33) A. In addition, a definitive agreement also contains provisions governing transaction structure/deal mechanics, pre-closing commitments (including covenants), termination provisions, and indemnifications

34) C. In a "one-step" merger transaction for public companies, target shareholders vote on whether to approve or reject the proposed transaction at a formal shareholder meeting pursuant to relevant state law. Prior to this meeting, a proxy statement is distributed to shareholders describing the transaction, parties involved, and other important information.

35) D. In Step I of the two-step process, the tender offer is made directly to the target's public shareholders with the target's approval pursuant to a definitive agreement. The tender offer is conditioned, among other things, on sufficient acceptances to ensure that the buyer will acquire a majority (or supermajority, as appropriate) of the target's shares within 20 business days of launching

the offer. If the requisite threshold of tendered shares is reached as designed (typically 90%), the acquirer can subsequently consummate a back-end "short form" merger (Step II) to squeeze out the remaining public shareholders without needing to obtain shareholder approval.

36)   C. In a squeeze out scenario, the entire process can be completed much quicker than in a one-step merger. If the requisite level of shares are tendered, the merger becomes effective shortly afterward (e.g., the same day or within a couple of days). In total, the transaction can be completed in as few as five weeks.

37)   Pros:
      ▪ Maximizes potential competitive dynamics and probability of achieving maximum sale price

      ▪ Helps to ensure that all likely bidders are approached

      Cons:
      ▪ Difficult to preserve confidentiality

      ▪ Unsuccessful outcome can create perception of an undesirable asset ("taint")

38)   A targeted auction is more appropriate if there is a select group of clearly defined buyers; also may be preferable if the seller wants to preserve confidentiality both externally and internally.

39)   Given the high stakes involved in an M&A transaction, companies need the specialized skills of investment bankers. For example, sell-side advisors have buyer relationships, sector knowledge, modeling and valuation expertise, execution experience, and dedicated resources.

40)   When there is a clear, natural buyer with synergies, who is prepared to launch a preemptive bid.

41)   Targeted auction = 5 to 15. Broad auction = 10 to 100+.

42)   Organization and preparation; First round; Second round; Negotiations; Closing

43)   First round refers to the time from the initial contacting of buyers to receipt of initial bids. Second round refers to the time from the management presentation to receipt of final bids.

44) Financial projections provide the foundation for the buy-side valuation work. They need to be realistic and defensible.

45) The teaser is generally a brief one- or two-page synopsis of the target, including a company overview, investment highlights, and summary financial information. It also contains contact information for the bankers running the sell-side process so that interested parties may respond.

46) The teaser is distributed at the start of the first round after the initial contact is made.

47) The CIM is distributed in the first round. The key gating item is the execution of the confidentiality agreement.

48) Data rooms generally contain a broad base of essential company information, documentation, and analyses. In essence, the data room is designed to provide a comprehensive set of information relevant for buyers to make an informed investment decision about the target, such as detailed financial reports, industry reports, and consulting studies. It also contains detailed company-specific information such as customer and supplier lists, labor contracts, purchase contracts, description and terms of outstanding debt, lease and pension contracts, and environmental compliance certification

49) The management presentation is a critical component of second round buyer due diligence. It provides a detailed overview of the target and interactive session with the management team. The core team presenting typically consists of the target's CEO, CFO, and key division heads or other operational executives, as appropriate.

50) Buyer due diligence is comprehensive data gathering, analysis, and assessment to fully understand the investment opportunity represented by the target. It consists of management presentations, site visits, studying the data room, and follow-up inquiries.

CHAPTER 7

Buy-Side M&A

1) Using the assumptions below, calculate ValueCo's equity purchase price and enterprise value

($ in millions, except per share data; shares in millions)

Assumptions	
ValueCo Current Share Price	$43.50
Premium to Current Share Price	35.0%
Fully Diluted Shares Outstanding	80.0
Total Debt	1,500.0
Cash and Cash Equivalents	250.0

a. Calculate equity purchase price

_____

b. Calculate enterprise value

_____

2) Using the equity purchase price and enterprise value determined in the prior question, as well as the following assumptions, complete the sources and uses table below and answer the following questions

($ in millions, except per share data)

Assumptions	
BuyerCo Current Share Price	$70.00
Exchange Ratio	0.8x
BuyerCo 2012E EBITDA	$1,486.3
ValueCo 2012E EBITDA	725.0
Synergies	100.0
Cash on Hand (to be used in transaction)	300.0
Tender / Call Premiums	20.0
Transaction Fees	40.0
Debt Financing Fees	90.0
Incremental Senior Secured Leverage	0.95x
Incremental Senior Leverage	0.65x
Stock Consideration for Equity	50.0%

($ in millions)

Sources of Funds			Uses of Funds	
Revolving Credit Facility			Purchase ValueCo Equity	
Term Loan B	A)		Repay Existing Debt	
Senior Notes	B)		Tender / Call Premiums	
Issuance of Common Stock	C)		Financing Fees	
Cash on Hand			Other Fees and Expenses	
Total Sources	D)		**Total Uses**	

a. Calculate the term loan B principal amount

b. Calculate the senior notes principal amount

c. Calculate the new common stock issued by BuyerCo

d. Determine the total sources amount

3) Using the purchase price and deal structure determined in the previous questions, as well as the following assumptions, complete the questions below regarding goodwill created, asset write-ups, and deferred tax liability

($ in millions)

Assumptions	
ValueCo Net Identifiable Assets	$2,500.0
Allocation of Purchase Price Premium to Tangible Assets	15.0%
Allocation of Purchase Price Premium to Intangible Assets	10.0%
BuyerCo Marginal Tax Rate	38.0%

($ in millions)

Goodwill Calculation	Allocation %	
Equity Purchase Price		
Less: ValueCo Net Identifiable Assets		
Total Allocable Purchase Premium		A)
Less: Tangible Asset Write-Up		B)
Less: Intangible Asset Write-Up		C)
Plus: Deferred Tax Liability		D)
Goodwill Created in Transaction		E)

a. Calculate the total allocable purchase price premium

_____

b. Calculate the tangible asset write-up amount

_____

c. Calculate the intangible asset write-up amount

_____

d. Calculate the deferred tax liability

_____

e. Determine the goodwill created in the transaction

_____

4) Given the sources & uses of funds determined in question #2, the goodwill created and asset write-ups determined in question #3, and the opening balance sheet below, complete the pro forma balance sheet at closing and answer the related questions (showing all adjustments)

($ in millions)

Balance Sheet

	BuyerCo 2012	ValueCo 2012	Adjustments +	-	Pro Forma 2012
Cash and Cash Equivalents	$400.0	$250.0			
Accounts Receivable	1,000.0	450.0			
Inventories	1,225.0	600.0			
Prepaids and Other Current Assets	525.0	175.0			
Total Current Assets	**$3,150.0**	**$1,475.0**			**A)**
Property, Plant and Equipment, net	2,500.0	2,500.0			**B)**
Goodwill	575.0	1,000.0			**C)**
Intangible Assets	825.0	875.0			**D)**
Other Assets	450.0	150.0			
Deferred Financing Fees	-	-			
Total Assets	**$7,500.0**	**$6,000.0**			
Accounts Payable	925.0	215.0			
Accrued Liabilities	945.0	275.0			
Other Current Liabilities	225.0	100.0			
Total Current Liabilities	**$2,095.0**	**$590.0**			
Revolving Credit Facility	-	-			
ValueCo Term Loan	-	1,000.0			
New Term Loan B	-	-			
BuyerCo Senior Notes	2,200.0	-			
ValueCo Senior Notes	-	500.0			
New Senior Notes	-	-			
Deferred Income Taxes	100.0	300.0			**E)**
Other Long-Term Liabilities	625.0	110.0			
Total Liabilities	**$5,020**	**$2,500**			
Noncontrolling Interests	-	-			
Shareholders' Equity	2,480.0	3,500.0			**F)**
Total Shareholders' Equity	**$2,480.0**	**$3,500.0**			
Total Liabilities and Equity	**$7,500.0**	**$6,000.0**			**G)**

Balance Check   *0.000*   *0.000*   *0.000*

    a. Calculate pro forma combined current assets

---

    b. Calculate pro forma combined PP&E

---

    c. Calculate pro forma combined goodwill

---

    d. Calculate pro forma combined intangible assets

---

    e. Calculate pro forma combined deferred income taxes

---

    f. Calculate pro forma combined shareholders' equity

---

    g. Calculate pro forma combined total liabilities and equity

---

5) Using the calculations performed in the previous questions, as well as the assumptions below, complete the accretion/(dilution) analysis for BuyerCo

Assumptions	
BuyerCo Marginal Tax Rate	38.0%
Tangible Asset Write-Up Depreciation Period	15 years
Intangible Asset Write-Up Amortization Period	15 years

($ in millions, except per share data)

Accretion / (Dilution) Analysis - 50% Stock / 50% Cash Consideration

	Pro forma	Projection Period				
		1	2	3	4	5
	2012	2013	2014	2015	2016	2017
BuyerCo EBIT	$1,317.4	$1,409.6	$1,494.2	$1,568.9	$1,631.6	$1,680.6
ValueCo EBIT	518.0	556.9	590.3	619.8	644.6	663.9
Synergies	100.0	100.0	100.0	100.0	100.0	100.0
Pro Forma Combined EBIT (pre-transaction)	**$1,935.4**	**$2,066.4**	**$2,184.4**	**$2,288.7**	**$2,376.2**	**$2,444.5**
Depreciation from Write-Up	A)					
Amortization from Write-Up	B)					
Pro Forma Combined EBIT						
Standalone Net Interest Expense	142.4	140.6	137.0	133.0	128.9	124.5
Incremental Net Interest Expense	230.9	206.4	158.0	132.8	130.8	128.6
Earnings Before Taxes						
Income Tax Expense						
Pro Forma Combined Net Income	**$945.8**	**$1,043.3**	**$1,148.7**	**$1,231.4**	**$1,289.5**	**$1,336.0**
BuyerCo Standalone Net Income	**$728.5**	**$786.8**	**$841.5**	**$890.2**	**$931.7**	**$964.8**
Standalone Fully Diluted Shares Outstanding	140.0	140.0	140.0	140.0	140.0	140.0
Net New Shares Issued in Transaction	33.6	33.6	33.6	33.6	33.6	33.6
Pro Forma Fully Diluted Shares Outstanding	**173.6**	**173.6**	**173.6**	**173.6**	**173.6**	**173.6**
Pro Forma Combined Diluted EPS		C)				
BuyerCo Standalone Diluted EPS			D)			
Accretion / (Dilution) - $				E)		
Accretion / (Dilution) - %					F)	
Accretive / Dilutive						
Included Pre-Tax Synergies						
Additional Pre-Tax Synergies to Breakeven						G)
Required Synergies to Breakeven / (Cushion)						

a. Calculate pro forma 2012 depreciation on the tangible asset write-up. Assume this amount is held constant throughout the projection period

b. Calculate pro forma 2012 amortization on the intangible asset write-up. Assume this amount is held constant throughout the projection period

    c. Calculate pro forma 2013 combined diluted EPS

    d. Calculate BuyerCo 2014 standalone diluted EPS

    e. Calculate 2015 accretion/(dilution) on a dollar amount basis

    f. Calculate 2016 accretion/(dilution) on a percentage basis

    g. Calculate 2017 additional pre-tax synergies to breakeven

6) If the pro forma EPS of two combined companies is higher than the EPS of the acquirer on a standalone basis, the transaction is said to be

    A. Accretive
    B. Dilutive
    C. Breakeven
    D. Consensus

7) If the pro forma EPS of two combined companies is lower than the standalone EPS of the acquirer, the transaction is said to be

    A. Accretive
    B. Dilutive
    C. Breakeven
    D. Consensus

Use the information below for the following three questions

($ in millions)	
Assumptions	
Pro Forma Combined Net Income	$1,000.0
Acquirer Standalone Net Income	700.0
Acquirer Standalone Fully Diluted Shares	200.0
Net New Shares Issued in Transaction	50.0
Tax Rate	38.0%

8) Calculate pro forma combined EPS

    A. $2.80
    B. $3.50
    C. $4.00
    D. $5.00

9) Calculate the accretion/(dilution) on a dollar amount basis

    A. ($0.50)
    B. $0.50
    C. ($0.88)
    D. $0.88

10) Calculate the accretion/(dilution) on a percentage basis

    A. (14.3%)
    B. 14.3%
    C. (12.5%)
    D. 12.5%

11) Calculate the breakeven pre-tax synergies / (cushion)

    A. ($161.3) million
    B. $161.3 million
    C. ($201.6) million
    D. $201.6 million

Use the information below for the following three questions

($ in millions)	
Assumptions	
Pro Forma Combined Net Income	$2,500.0
Acquirer Standalone Net Income	1,800.0
Standalone Fully Diluted Shares Outstanding	300.0
Net New Shares Issued in Transaction	135.0
Tax Rate	38.0%

12) Calculate pro forma combined EPS

    A. $4.14
    B. $5.75
    C. $7.15
    D. $8.33

13) Calculate the accretion/(dilution) on a dollar amount basis

    A. ($0.25)
    B. $0.25
    C. ($0.40)
    D. $0.40

14) Calculate the accretion/(dilution) on a percentage basis

    A. (4.2%)
    B. 4.2%
    C. (4.4%)
    D. 4.4%

15) Calculate the breakeven pre-tax synergies/(cushion)

    A. ($122.4) million
    B. $122.4 million
    C. ($177.4) million
    D. $177.4 million

16) Assuming all else being equal, if a company with a P/E of 15x acquires a company with a P/E of 12x in an all-stock deal, the transaction is _____?

    A. Accretive
    B. Dilutive
    C. Breakeven
    D. Cannot be determined

17) Assuming all else being equal, if a company with a P/E of 12x acquires a company with a P/E of 15x in an all-stock deal, the transaction is _____?

    A. Accretive
    B. Dilutive
    C. Breakeven
    D. Cannot be determined

18) An accretion/(dilution) analysis is typically performed by

    A. Public strategic buyers
    B. Sponsor buyers
    C. Family-owned sellers
    D. Non-public foreign buyers

19) Which of the following are common types of synergies realized in M&A transactions?

    I. Merger
    II. Revenue
    III. Cost
    IV. Stock

    A. I and II
    B. II and III
    C. III and IV
    D. II, III, and IV

20) Which Internal Revenue Code governs net operating losses?

    A. Section 302
    B. Section 330
    C. Section 382
    D. Section 389

21) Which of the following is NOT a potential "source" of funds for consummating a deal?

    A. New stock issued
    B. Cash on balance sheet of buyer
    C. Equity value of seller
    D. Preferred stock issued

22) The excess paid for a target over its identifiable net asset value is known as

   A. Brand premium
   B. Goodwill
   C. Intangible value
   D. Tangible value

23) Using the information below, calculate the allocable purchase premium

   ($ in millions)

Assumptions	
Equity Purchase Price	$3,000.0
Shareholders' Equity	2,000.0
Existing Goodwill	750.0

   A. $1,250.0 million
   B. $1,750.0 million
   C. $5,000.0 million
   D. $5,750.0 million

24) Debt financing fees in an M&A deal are

   A. Expensed immediately
   B. Capitalized
   C. Written off
   D. Not applicable

25) A transaction where the buyer purchases all assets & liabilities of the seller is known as

   A. Asset purchase
   B. Stock purchase
   C. Section 308 election
   D. Section 382 purchase

26) A transaction where the buyer purchases certain assets and assumes only certain liabilities is known as

   A. Asset purchase
   B. Stock purchase
   C. Section 338 (h)(10) election
   D. Section 382 purchase

27) Why might a buyer prefer an asset sale to a stock sale?

    A. Can potentially use the seller's NOLs
    B. Less complex than stock sale
    C. Benefits from tax shield
    D. Creates deferred tax assets

28) A Section 338(h)(10) election is legally a/an _____ purchase, but for accounting purposes it is treated like a/an _____ purchase.

    A. stock; asset
    B. asset; stock
    C. stock; tax-free
    D. asset; tax-free

29) What is a greenfield?

    A. Building a new factory from scratch
    B. Modifying /upgrading a preexisting factory
    C. Antitakeover method where the target purchases shares at a premium from a potential buyer to halt an unfriendly takeover
    D. Integrating a newly purchased company quickly and efficiently

30) All of the following are reasons why a company would choose to grow through acquisitions as opposed to greenfielding EXCEPT

    A. Less risky
    B. Less expensive
    C. Premiums typically associated with acquisitions
    D. Longer time required to greenfield

31) What are economies of scale?

    A. Company's ability to integrate a new acquisition
    B. Company's ability to enter into a new geography due to an acquisition
    C. Producing and selling more units at a higher cost per unit
    D. Producing and selling more units at a lower cost per unit

32) What are economies of scope?

    A. Allocating resources across multiple products
    B. Consolidating resources to focus on one central product
    C. Company's ability to purchase smaller targets due to its size
    D. Company's ability to sell products in several countries

33) All of the following are common acquisitions strategies EXCEPT

    A. Horizontal integration
    B. Vertical integration
    C. Six Sigma
    D. Conglomeration

34) An example of backward integration is a

    A. Distributor acquiring a supplier
    B. Manufacturer acquiring a distributor
    C. Supplier acquiring another supplier
    D. Manufacturer entering into distribution through greenfielding

35) An example of forward integration is a

    A. Manufacturer acquiring a supplier
    B. Supplier acquiring a distributor
    C. Distributor acquiring another distributor
    D. Manufacturer entering into distribution through greenfielding

36) What is conglomeration?

    A. Corporation that is the largest amongst its competitors
    B. Corporation that sells its products and services in several countries
    C. Acquisition strategy whereby a company makes acquisitions in relatively unrelated business areas
    D. Acquisition strategy whereby a company makes acquisitions within one business area

37) All of the following are common forms of M&A financing EXCEPT

    A. Equity
    B. Current assets
    C. Debt
    D. Cash on hand

38) Consideration for merger-of-equals transactions typically are _____ and the premium is _____ compared to a takeover premium.

   A. All-stock; small
   B. All-stock; high
   C. All-cash; the same
   D. All-cash; high

39) All of the following are potential disadvantages of using equity for M&A financing EXCEPT

   A. Shareholder vote needed if 20% or greater of outstanding shares are issued in a transaction
   B. Price volatility of buyer's stock
   C. Target shareholders often prefer cash
   D. Rating agency views

40) All of the following are conduit entities where corporate earnings are passed on directly to shareholders and not taxed at the corporate level EXCEPT

   A. S Corp
   B. C Corp
   C. LLC
   D. Partnership

41) Representations and warranties do not survive closing for which of the following

   A. Family-owned company
   B. Public company
   C. Sponsor-owned company
   D. Reps and warranties always survive

42) Deferred tax liabilities are calculated as

   A. Goodwill less PP&E
   B. PP&E multiplied by the acquirer's tax rate
   C. Tangible and intangible asset write-ups multiplied by the acquirer's tax rate
   D. Goodwill multiplied by the acquirer's tax rate

43) Why is a deferred tax liability created?

    A. Stepped-up assets are depreciated for tax purposes but not on a GAAP book basis

    B. Stepped-up assets are depreciated on a GAAP book basis but not for tax purposes

    C. Stepped-up assets are depreciated faster on a GAAP book basis than for tax purposes

    D. Different tax rates among the acquirer and target

44) What type of deal is most common for C Corps?

    A. Section 338(h)(10) election

    B. Merger-of-equals

    C. Stock sale

    D. Asset sale

45) What does a company's "inside basis" refer to?

    A. Tax basis of its stock

    B. Tax basis of its public shareholders

    C. Tax basis of its assets

    D. Tax basis of the management team's stock holdings

46) What does a company's "outside basis" refer to?

    A. Tax basis of its stock

    B. Tax basis of its public shareholders

    C. Tax basis of its assets

    D. Tax basis of the management team's stock holdings

47) A Section 338(h)(10) election is most common for

    A. Large public companies

    B. C Corps

    C. Foreign companies

    D. Corporate subsidiaries

48) What does the "election" component of a Section 338(h)(10) election refer to?

   A. Buyer's decision to pursue a 338(h)(10) election is subject to a shareholder vote
   B. Buyer's decision to pursue a 338(h)(10) election is subject to a Board of Directors vote regardless of size
   C. Buyer can elect to do a 338(h)(10) election on its own
   D. Both buyer and seller need to consent to the 338 (h)(10) election

49) In a corporate stock sale, the selling entity is

   A. The corporate entity
   B. The company's shareholders
   C. Stock exchange where the corporation is listed
   D. A foreign subsidiary

50) In an asset sale, the selling entity is

   A. The corporate entity
   B. The company's shareholders
   C. Asset-based lending facility
   D. HoldCo

51) Which deal structure risks double taxation in the event proceeds are distributed to shareholders

   A. Stock sale
   B. Asset sale
   C. S Corp
   D. C Corp

52) Contribution analysis is most appropriate for

   A. Merger-of-equals deals
   B. LBOs
   C. Take-private deals
   D. Equity financing

53) Which of the following serve to reduce goodwill created in an M&A transaction?

    A. Write-up of tangible assets
    B. Equity control premium
    C. DTLs
    D. Future synergies

54) All of the following reduce goodwill created in an M&A transaction EXCEPT

    A. Write-up of tangible assets
    B. Write-up of intangible assets
    C. Target net identifiable assets
    D. DTLs

55) Why would an acquirer increase the equity portion of its M&A financing?

    A. Improve accretion of the deal
    B. Improve pro forma credit statistics for the deal
    C. Increase return on equity
    D. Debt financing is more expensive than equity financing

56) What does accretion/(dilution) analysis measure and what are its key drivers?

_____

_____

_____

_____

57) Under what circumstances might a buyer pursue an acquisition that isn't immediately accretive?

_____

_____

_____

_____

58) Why might a higher bid be rejected in favor of a lower one?

_____

_____

_____

_____

1) Calculation of equity purchase price and enterprise value

| = Offer Price per Share x Fully Diluted Shares |
| = $58.73 x 80.0 million shares |

($ in millions, except per share data; shares in millions)

Purchase Price	
Current Share Price	$43.50
Premium to Current Share Price	35.0%
Offer Price per Share	$58.73
Fully Diluted Shares	80.0
Equity Purchase Price	**$4,700.0**
Plus: Total Debt	1,500.0
Less: Cash and Equivalents	(250.0)
Enterprise Value	**$5,950.0**

| = Equity Value + Total Debt - Cash and Cash Equivalents |
| = $4,700.0 million + $1,500.0 million - $250.0 million |

    a. $4,700.0 million. Equity purchase price is calculated as offer price per share multiplied by fully diluted shares outstanding. ($58.73 × 80.0 million shares)

    b. $5,950.0 million. Enterprise value is calculated as equity value plus total debt less cash and cash equivalents. ($4,700.0 million + $1,500.0 million - $250.0 million)

2) Calculation of sources and uses

($ in millions)

Sources of Funds		Uses of Funds	
Revolving Credit Facility	-	Purchase ValueCo Equity	$4,700.0
Term Loan B	2,200.0	Repay Existing Debt	1,500.0
Senior Notes	1,500.0	Tender / Call Premiums	20.0
Issuance of Common Stock	2,350.0	Financing Fees	40.0
Cash on Hand	300.0	Other Fees and Expenses	90.0
Total Sources	**6,350.00**	**Total Uses**	**$6,350.0**

    a. $2,200.0 million. The term loan B principal amount is calculated as pro forma combined 2012E EBITDA multiplied by the additional senior secured leverage. Pro forma combined EBITDA is the sum of BuyerCo 2012E EBITDA, ValueCo 2012E EBITDA, and synergies

($ in millions)

Calculation of Term Loan B Principal Amount	
BuyerCo 2012E EBITDA	$1,486.3
ValueCo 2012E EBITDA	725.0
Synergies	100.0
Pro Forma Combined 2012E EBITDA	**$2,311.3**
Incremental Senior Secured Leverage	0.95x
Term Loan B Principal Amount	**$2,200.0**

b. $1,500.0 million. The senior notes principal amount is calculated as pro forma combined 2012E EBITDA multiplied by the senior secured leverage.

($ in millions)

Calculation of Senior Notes Principal Amount	
Pro Forma Combined 2012E EBITDA	$2,311.3
Incremental Senior Leverage	0.65x
Senior Notes Principal Amount	**$1,500.0**

c. $2,350.0 million. New common stock issued is calculated as equity purchase price multiplied by the stock consideration for equity.

($ in millions)

Calculation of New Common Stock Issued	
Equity Purchase Price	$4,700.0
Stock Consideration for Equity	50.0%
New Common Stock Issued	**$2,350.0**

d. $6,350.0 million. Total sources is calculated as the sum of term loan B, senior notes, the issuance of common stock, and cash on hand.

($ in millions)

Calculation of Total Sources	
Term Loan B	$2,200.0
Senior Notes	1,500.0
Issuance of Common Stock	2,350.0
Cash on Hand	300.0
Total Sources	**$6,350.0**

3) Goodwill created, asset write-ups, and deferred tax liability

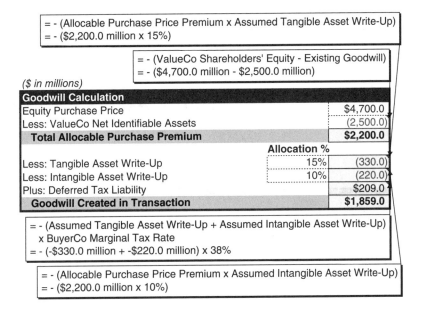

a. $2,200.0 million. The total allocable purchase price premium is calculated as equity purchase price less ValueCo net identifiable assets. ($4,700.0 million - $2,500.0 million)

b. ($330.0) million. The tangible asset write-up amount is calculated as the total allocable purchase premium multiplied by the assumed tangible asset write-up. ($2,200.0 million × 15%)

c. ($220.0) million. The intangible asset write-up amount is calculated as the total allocable purchase premium multiplied by the assumed intangible asset write-up. ($2,200.0 million × 10%)

d. $209.0 million. The deferred tax liability is calculated as the sum of the tangible and intangible write-ups multiplied by BuyerCo's marginal tax rate. ($550.0 million × 38%)

e. $1,859.0 million. The goodwill created in the transaction is calculated as the total allocable purchase premium less the tangible and intangible write-ups plus the deferred tax liability created in the transaction. ($2,200.0 million - $330.0 million - $220.0 million + $209.0 million)

4) Balance sheet adjustments

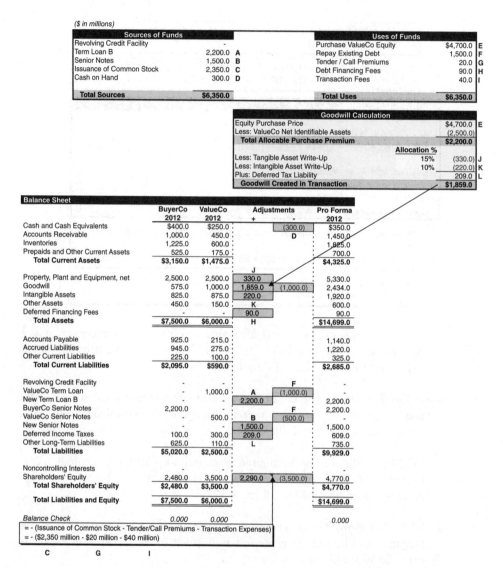

($ in millions)

Sources of Funds		
Revolving Credit Facility	-	
Term Loan B	2,200.0	A
Senior Notes	1,500.0	B
Issuance of Common Stock	2,350.0	C
Cash on Hand	300.0	D
Total Sources	**$6,350.0**	

Uses of Funds		
Purchase ValueCo Equity	$4,700.0	E
Repay Existing Debt	1,500.0	F
Tender / Call Premiums	20.0	G
Debt Financing Fees	90.0	H
Transaction Fees	40.0	I
Total Uses	**$6,350.0**	

Goodwill Calculation		
Equity Purchase Price	$4,700.0	E
Less: ValueCo Net Identifiable Assets	(2,500.0)	
Total Allocable Purchase Premium	**$2,200.0**	
	Allocation %	
Less: Tangible Asset Write-Up	15%	(330.0) J
Less: Intangible Asset Write-Up	10%	(220.0) K
Plus: Deferred Tax Liability		209.0 L
Goodwill Created in Transaction		**$1,859.0**

Balance Sheet	BuyerCo 2012	ValueCo 2012	Adjustments +	Adjustments -	Pro Forma 2012
Cash and Cash Equivalents	$400.0	$250.0		(300.0)	$350.0
Accounts Receivable	1,000.0	450.0		D	1,450.0
Inventories	1,225.0	600.0			1,825.0
Prepaids and Other Current Assets	525.0	175.0			700.0
Total Current Assets	**$3,150.0**	**$1,475.0**			**$4,325.0**
			J		
Property, Plant and Equipment, net	2,500.0	2,500.0	330.0		5,330.0
Goodwill	575.0	1,000.0	1,859.0	(1,000.0)	2,434.0
Intangible Assets	825.0	875.0	220.0		1,920.0
Other Assets	450.0	150.0	K		600.0
Deferred Financing Fees	-	-	90.0		90.0
Total Assets	**$7,500.0**	**$6,000.0**	H		**$14,699.0**
Accounts Payable	925.0	215.0			1,140.0
Accrued Liabilities	945.0	275.0			1,220.0
Other Current Liabilities	225.0	100.0			325.0
Total Current Liabilities	**$2,095.0**	**$590.0**			**$2,685.0**
Revolving Credit Facility	-	-	F		-
ValueCo Term Loan	-	1,000.0	A	(1,000.0)	-
New Term Loan B	-	-	2,200.0		2,200.0
BuyerCo Senior Notes	2,200.0	-			2,200.0
ValueCo Senior Notes	-	500.0	B	(500.0)	-
New Senior Notes	-	-	1,500.0		1,500.0
Deferred Income Taxes	100.0	300.0	209.0		609.0
Other Long-Term Liabilities	625.0	110.0	L		735.0
Total Liabilities	**$5,020.0**	**$2,500.0**			**$9,929.0**
Noncontrolling Interests	-	-			-
Shareholders' Equity	2,480.0	3,500.0	2,290.0	(3,500.0)	4,770.0
Total Shareholders' Equity	**$2,480.0**	**$3,500.0**			**$4,770.0**
Total Liabilities and Equity	**$7,500.0**	**$6,000.0**			**$14,699.0**
Balance Check	0.000	0.000			0.000

= - (Issuance of Common Stock - Tender/Call Premiums - Transaction Expenses)
= - ($2,350 million - $20 million - $40 million)

  C   G   I

a. $4,325.0 million. Pro forma combined current assets is calculated as the sum of cash and cash equivalents, accounts receivable, inventories, and prepaids and other current assets. ($350.0 million + $1,450.0 million + $1,825.0 million + $700.0 million)

b. $5,330.0 million. Pro forma combined PP&E is calculated as the sum of BuyerCo's and ValueCo's PP&E, plus the additional tangible asset write-up. ($2,500.0 million + $2,500.0 million + $330.0 million)

c. $2,434.0 million. Pro forma combined goodwill is calculated as the sum of BuyerCo's and ValueCo's existing goodwill, plus the additional goodwill created in the transaction, less ValueCo's goodwill. ($575.0 million + $1,000.0 million + $1,859.0 million - $1,000.0 million)

d. $1,920.0 million. Pro forma combined intangible assets are calculated as the sum of BuyerCo's and ValueCo's intangible assets, plus the additional intangible asset write-up. ($825.0 million + $875.0 million + $220.0 million)

e. $609.0 million. Pro forma combined deferred income taxes are calculated as the sum of BuyerCo's and ValueCo's existing deferred income taxes, plus the additional deferred tax liability created in the transaction. ($100.0 million + $300.0 million + $209.0 million)

f. $4,770.0 million. Pro forma combined shareholders' equity is calculated as the sum of BuyerCo's existing shareholders' equity, plus the issuance of common stock, less tender/call premiums, and transaction expenses. ($2,480.0 million + $2,350.0 million - $20.0 million - $40.0 million)

g. $14,699.0 million. Pro forma combined total liabilities and equity is the sum of pro forma combined total liabilities and pro forma combined total shareholders' equity. ($9,929.0 million + $4,770.0 million)

5) Accretion/(dilution) analysis

> = Intangible Asset Write-up / Amortization Period
> = $220.0 million / 15 years

> = Tangible Asset Write-up / Depreciation Period
> = $330.0 million / 15 years

($ in millions, except per share data)

Accretion / (Dilution) Analysis - 50% Stock / 50% Cash Consideration

	Pro forma	Projection Period				
		1	2	3	4	5
	2012	2013	2014	2015	2016	2017
BuyerCo EBIT	$1,317.4	$1,409.6	$1,494.2	$1,568.9	$1,631.6	$1,680.6
ValueCo EBIT	518.0	556.9	590.3	619.8	644.6	663.9
Synergies	100.0	100.0	100.0	100.0	100.0	100.0
Pro Forma Combined EBIT (pre-transaction)	**$1,935.4**	**$2,066.4**	**$2,184.4**	**$2,288.7**	**$2,376.2**	**$2,444.5**
Depreciation from Write-Up	22.0	22.0	22.0	22.0	22.0	22.0
Amortization from Write-Up	14.7	14.7	14.7	14.7	14.7	14.7
Pro Forma Combined EBIT	**$1,898.7**	**$2,029.8**	**$2,147.8**	**$2,252.0**	**$2,339.5**	**$2,407.8**
Standalone Net Interest Expense	142.4	140.6	137.0	133.0	128.9	124.5
Incremental Net Interest Expense	230.9	206.4	158.0	132.8	130.8	128.6
Earnings Before Taxes	**$1,525.4**	**$1,682.7**	**$1,852.8**	**$1,986.1**	**$2,079.9**	**$2,154.8**
Income Tax Expense @ 38.0%	579.7	639.4	704.0	754.7	790.4	818.8
Pro Forma Combined Net Income	**$945.8**	**$1,043.3**	**$1,148.7**	**$1,231.4**	**$1,289.5**	**$1,336.0**
BuyerCo Standalone Net Incom	**$728.5**	**$786.8**	**$841.5**	**$890.2**	**$931.7**	**$964.8**
Standalone Fully Diluted Shares Outstanding	140.0	140.0	140.0	140.0	140.0	140.0
Net New Shares Issued in Transaction	33.6	33.6	33.6	33.6	33.6	33.6
Pro Forma Fully Diluted Shares Outstanding	**173.6**	**173.6**	**173.6**	**173.6**	**173.6**	**173.6**
Pro Forma Combined Diluted EPS	$5.45	$6.01	$6.62	$7.09	$7.43	$7.70
BuyerCo Standalone Diluted EPS	5.20	5.62	6.01	6.36	6.66	6.89
Accretion / (Dilution) - $	**$0.25**	**$0.39**	**$0.61**	**$0.74**	**$0.77**	**$0.81**
Accretion / (Dilution) - %	**4.7%**	**7.0%**	**10.1%**	**11.6%**	**11.6%**	**11.7%**
Accretive / Dilutive	*Accretive*	*Accretive*	*Accretive*	*Accretive*	*Accretive*	*Accretive*
Included Pre-Tax Synergies	$100.0	$100.0	$100.0	$100.0	$100.0	$100.0
Additional Pre-Tax Synergies to Breakeven	(68.7)	(109.5)	(170.1)	(205.9)	(216.8)	(225.5)
Required Synergies to Breakeven / (Cushion)	**$31.3**	**($9.5)**	**($70.1)**	**($105.9)**	**($116.8)**	**($125.5)**

> = Pro Forma Net Income$_{2013E}$ / Pro Forma Fully Diluted Shares$_{2013E}$
> = $1,043.3 million / 173.6 million

> = BuyerCo Standalone Net Income$_{2014E}$ / Standalone Fully Diluted Shares
> = $841.5 million / 140.0 million

> = Pro Forma Combined Diluted EPS$_{2015E}$ - BuyerCo Standalone Diluted EPS$_{2015E}$
> = $7.09 - $6.36

> = Pro Forma Combined Diluted EPS$_{2016E}$ / BuyerCo Standalone Diluted EPS$_{2016E}$ - 1
> = $7.43 / $6.66 - 1

> = - (EPS Accretion/(Dilution)$_{2017E}$ x Pro Forma Fully Diluted Shares) / (1 - Tax Rate)
> = - ($0.81 x 173.6 million / (1 - 38%)

a. $22.0 million. Pro forma 2012 depreciation on the tangible asset write-up is calculated as the tangible asset write-up divided by the depreciation period. ($330.0 million / 15 years)

b. $14.7 million. Pro forma 2012 amortization on the intangible asset write-up is calculated as the intangible asset write-up divided by the amortization period. ($220.0 million / 15 years)

c. $6.01. Pro forma 2013 combined diluted EPS is calculated as pro forma 2013 combined net income divided by pro forma 2013 fully diluted shares outstanding. ($1,043.3 million / 173.6 million shares).

d. $6.01. BuyerCo 2014 standalone diluted EPS is calculated as BuyerCo standalone net income divided by standalone fully diluted shares outstanding. ($841.5 million / 140.0 million shares).

e. $0.74. 2015 accretion/(dilution) on a dollar amount basis is calculated as pro forma 2015 combined diluted EPS less BuyerCo 2015 standalone diluted EPS. ($7.09 - $6.36)

f. 11.6%. 2016 accretion/(dilution) on a percentage basis is calculated as pro forma 2016 combined diluted EPS divided by BuyerCo 2016 standalone diluted EPS, less 1. (($7.43 / $6.66) - 1)

g. ($225.6) million. 2017 additional pre-tax synergies to breakeven is calculated with the formula (-EPS accretion/(dilution) × pro forma fully diluted shares) / (1 - tax rate)). (-$0.81 × 173.6 million / (1 - 38%)).

6) A. Public strategic buyers use accretion/(dilution) analysis to measure the pro forma effects of a transaction on earnings, assuming a given purchase price and financing structure. The acquirer's EPS pro forma for the transaction is compared to its EPS on a standalone basis. If the pro forma EPS is higher than the standalone EPS, the transaction is said to be accretive; conversely, if the pro forma EPS is lower, the transaction is said to be dilutive.

7) B. If the pro forma EPS is lower than the standalone EPS, the transaction is said to be dilutive.

8) C. Pro forma combined diluted EPS is found by dividing the pro forma combined net income by the pro forma fully diluted shares outstanding.

> = Pro Forma Net Income / Pro Forma Fully Diluted Shares
> = $1,000.0 million / 250.0 million

($ in millions, except per share data)

Accretion / (Dilution) Analysis	
Pro Forma Combined Net Income	**$1,000.0**
Acquirer Standalone Net Income	**700.0**
Standalone Fully Diluted Shares Outstanding	200.0
Net New Shares Issued in Transaction	50.0
Pro Forma Fully Diluted Shares Outstanding	**250.0**
Pro Forma Combined Diluted EPS	$4.00
Acquirer Standalone Diluted EPS	3.50
Accretion / (Dilution) - $	**$0.50**
Accretion / (Dilution) - %	**14.3%**
Accretive / Dilutive	*Accretive*
Required Synergies to Breakeven / (Cushion)	**($201.6)**

> = - (EPS Accretion/(Dilution) x Pro Forma Fully Diluted Shares) / (1 - Tax Rate)
> = - ($0.50 x 260.0 million / (1 - 38%)

> = Pro Forma Combined Diluted EPS / BuyerCo Standalone Diluted EPS - 1
> = $4.00 / $3.50 - 1

> = Pro Forma Combined Diluted EPS - BuyerCo Standalone Diluted EPS
> = $4.00 - $3.50

9) B. Accretion/(dilution) on a dollar amount basis is calculated by subtracting the pro forma combined EPS by the acquirer's standalone diluted EPS. As shown above, the transaction is accretive on a dollar amount basis by $0.50.

10) B. Accretion/(dilution) on a percentage basis is calculated by dividing the pro forma combined EPS by the acquirer's standalone diluted EPS, and subtracting 1. As shown above the transaction is accretive on a percentage basis by 14.3%.

11) C. As shown above, breakeven pre-tax synergies/(cushion) is calculated with the formula: (- (EPS accretion/(dilution) × pro forma fully diluted shares) / (1 - tax rate)). Since the transaction is accretive, the analysis determines the synergy cushion before the transaction becomes dilutive.

12) B. As shown below, the pro forma combined diluted EPS is found by dividing the pro forma combined net income by the pro forma fully diluted shares outstanding.

= Pro Forma Net Income / Pro Forma Fully Diluted Shares
= $2,500.0 million / 435.0 million

($ in millions, except per share data)

Accretion / (Dilution) Analysis	
Pro Forma Combined Net Income	**$2,500.0**
Acquirer Standalone Net Income	**1,800.0**
Standalone Fully Diluted Shares Outstanding	300.0
Net New Shares Issued in Transaction	135.0
Pro Forma Fully Diluted Shares Outstanding	**435.0**
Pro Forma Combined Diluted EPS	$5.75
Acquirer Standalone Diluted EPS	6.00
Accretion / (Dilution) - $	**($0.25)**
Accretion / (Dilution) - %	**(4.2%)**
Accretive / Dilutive	*Dilutive*
Required Synergies to Breakeven / (Cushion)	**$177.4**

= - (EPS Accretion/(Dilution) x Pro Forma Fully Diluted Shares) / (1 - Tax Rate)
= - (-$0.25 x 435.0 million / (1 - 38%)

= Pro Forma Combined Diluted EPS / BuyerCo Standalone Diluted EPS - 1
= $5.75 / $6.00 - 1

= Pro Forma Combined Diluted EPS - BuyerCo Standalone Diluted EPS
= $5.75 - $6.00

13) A. As shown above, the transaction is dilutive on a dollar amount basis by ($0.25).

14) A. As shown above, the transaction is dilutive on a percentage basis by (4.2%).

15) D. As shown above, the transaction is dilutive. Therefore, the analysis determines the amount of pre-tax synergies necessary to breakeven on an accretion/(dilution) basis.

16) A. In an all-stock deal, if an acquirer has a higher P/E than the seller, the deal is accretive.

17) B. In an all-stock deal, if an acquirer has a lower P/E than the seller, the deal is dilutive.

18) A. In addition to the standard valuation methodologies (comparable companies, precedent transactions, DCF, and LBO analysis) used to establish a valuation range for a potential acquisition, public strategic buyers also use

accretion/(dilution) analysis to measure the pro forma effects of a transaction on earnings, assuming a given purchase price and financing structure. It is often critical that a transaction needs to be accretive in order for the acquirer to agree to the deal.

19) B. Revenue and cost are the two types of potential synergies. Revenue synergies refer to new revenue streams (cross-selling, new distribution channels. etc.) available to the combined company. Cost synergies refer to cost-cutting initiatives (eliminating duplicate operations, employee redundancies, etc.) that can be achieved through the combination.

20) C. Section 382 of the Internal Revenue Code is centered on the limitation of net operating loss carryforwards and certain built-in losses following ownership change.

21) C. Equity value of the seller is a use, not a source, of funds.

22) B. Referred to as the "excess purchase price," goodwill is calculated as the purchase price minus the target's net identifiable assets after allocations to the target's tangible and intangible assets, plus the DTL.

23) B. Allocable purchase premium is calculated as equity purchase price less net identifiable assets.

($ in millions)	
Goodwill Calculation	
Equity Purchase Price	$3,000.0
Less: ValueCo Net Identifiable Assets	(1,250.0)
Total Allocable Purchase Premium	**$1,750.0**

= - (ValueCo Shareholders' Equity - Existing Goodwill)
= - ($2,000.0 million - $750.0 million)

24) B. Financing fees are capitalized on the buyer's balance sheet as an asset and are amortized over the life of the security. They are not expensed when they occur such as M&A fees in a transaction.

25) B. In a stock sale, the target ceases to remain in existence post-transaction, becoming a wholly-owned subsidiary of the acquirer. As a result, the acquirer assumes all of the target's past, present, and future known and unknown liabilities, in addition to the assets.

26) A. An asset sale refers to an M&A transaction whereby an acquirer purchases all or some of the target's assets. Under this structure, the target legally remains in existence post-transaction, which means that the buyer purchases specified assets and assumes certain liabilities. This can help alleviate the buyer's risk, especially when there may be substantial unknown contingent liabilities.

27) C. An asset sale may provide certain tax benefits for the buyer in the event it can "step up" the tax basis of the target's acquired assets to fair market value, as reflected in the purchase price. The stepped-up portion is depreciable and/ or amortizable on a tax deductible basis over the assets' useful life for both GAAP book and tax purposes. This results in real cash benefits for the buyer during the stepped-up depreciable period.

28) A. A 338(h)(10) election is treated like a stock purchase for legal purposes. However, it is treated like an asset purchase for accounting purposes. In a 338(h)(10) election, the buyer acquires all assets and liabilities of the seller (as in a stock purchase), but the buyer also receives a "step-up" so it can depreciate from a higher base (as in an asset purchase).

29) A. Greenfielding refers to building a new factory or facility from scratch.

30) C. In many instances, growth through an acquisition represents a cheaper, faster, and less risky option than greenfielding, building a business from scratch.

31) D. Economies of scale refer to the notion that larger companies are able to produce and sell more units at a lower cost per unit than smaller competitors. Larger companies are typically able to do this by purchasing materials in bulk, spreading marketing and administrative costs over a larger work force, and achieving lower financing fees.

32) A. Economics of scope refer to the allocation of common resources across multiple products and geographies. For example, if a company produces two or more similar products, they can spread costs over each of the different product lines.

33) C. Six Sigma is not an acquisition strategy. Developed by Motorola in 1986, Six Sigma began as a business strategy emphasizing reducing manufacturing defects and has since evolved into a management philosophy focused on quality control.

34) A. Backward integration is when companies move upstream to purchase their suppliers, such as a distributor acquiring a supplier.

35) B. Forward integration is when companies move downstream to purchase their customers, such as a supplier acquiring a distributor.

36) C. Conglomeration refers to an acquisition strategy that brings together companies that are generally unrelated in terms of products and services provided under one corporate umbrella. Two of the largest and most well-known conglomerates are General Electric and Berkshire Hathaway.

37) B. The central forms of M&A financing are cash on hand, debt financing, and equity financing. The acquirer typically chooses among the available sources of funds based on a variety of factors, including cost of capital, balance sheet flexibility, rating agency considerations, and speed and certainty to close the transaction.

38) A. For a merger-of-equals (MOE) M&A transaction, the consideration is typically all-stock and the premium received by the sellers is small relative to a takeover premium.

39) D. Rating agency views are not a disadvantage of using equity for M&A financing. Companies might elect to use more equity in M&A financing to ensure a given credit rating will be received or maintained.

40) B. A C Corp is a corporation that is taxed separately from its shareholders (i.e., at the corporate level only as opposed to the shareholder level). S Corps, LLCs or other partnerships, by contrast, are conduit entities in which corporate earnings are passed on directly to shareholders and therefore not taxed at the corporate level.

41) B. In a public company transaction, representations and warranties do not survive closing. In a private company transaction with a limited number of shareholders, however, representations and warranties typically survive closing with former shareholders providing indemnification to the acquirer.

42) C. In a stock sale, the transaction-related depreciation and amortization is not deductible for tax purposes. Neither buyer nor seller pays taxes on the "gain"

on the GAAP asset write-up. Therefore, from an IRS tax revenue generation standpoint, the buyer should not be allowed to reap future tax deduction benefits from this accounting convention. From an accounting perspective, this discrepancy between book and tax is resolved through the creation of a deferred tax liability on the balance sheet (where it often appears as deferred income taxes). The DTL is calculated as the amount of the write-up multiplied by the company's tax rate.

43) B. A deferred tax liability is created due to the fact that the target's written-up assets are depreciated on a GAAP book basis but not for tax purposes. Therefore, while the depreciation expense is netted out from pre-tax income on the GAAP income statement, the company does not receive cash benefits from the tax shield. In other words, the perceived tax shield on the book depreciation exists for accounting purposes only. In reality, the company must pay cash taxes on the pre-tax income amount before the deduction of transaction-related depreciation and amortization expense.

44) C. Stock deals are the most common structure for C Corps.

45) C. Tax basis of a company's assets is known as "inside basis."

46) A. Tax basis of a company's stock is known as "outside basis."

47) D. 338(h)(10) election is commonly used when the target is a subsidiary of a parent corporation. In a subsidiary sale, the parent typically pays taxes on the gain on sale at the corporate tax rate regardless of whether it is a stock sale, asset sale, or 338(h)(10) election.

48) D. The "election" component of a 338(h)(10) election refers to the fact that the transaction must be explicitly consented to by both the buyer and seller. In this scenario, typically the buyer is willing to pay the seller a higher price in return for acquiescing to a 338(h)(10) election, which affords tax benefits to the buyer from the asset step-up that results in the creation of tax-deductible depreciation and amortization. This results in a lower after-tax cost for the acquirer and greater after-tax proceeds for the seller. The Internal Revenue Code requires that the 338(h)(10) be a joint election by both the buyer and seller, and therefore forces both parties to work together to maximize the value.

49) B. A stock sale involves the acquirer purchasing the target's stock from the company's shareholders for some form of consideration. From a tax perspective,

in the event that target shareholders receive significant equity consideration in the acquirer, their capital gain is generally deferred. On the other hand, in the event they receive cash, a capital gain is triggered. The extent to which a capital gains tax is triggered is dependent upon whether the shareholder is taxable (e.g., an individual) or non-taxable (e.g., a pension fund).

50) A. The corporate entity itself is the selling entity in an asset sale. Under this structure, the target legally remains in existence post-transaction, which means that the buyer purchases specified assets and assumes certain liabilities.

51) B. In an asset sale, double taxation for a subsidiary sale occurs in the event sale proceeds are distributed to shareholders.

52) A. Contribution analysis, which depicts the financial "contributions" that each party makes to the pro forma entity in terms of sales, EBITDA, EBIT, net income, and equity value, is commonly used in merger-of-equals transactions.

53) A. Write-ups of a company's tangible and intangible assets reduce the amount of goodwill created in an M&A transaction. Goodwill is calculated as the purchase price minus the target's net identifiable assets after allocations to the target's tangible and intangible assets, plus the DTL.

54) D. DTLs get added to goodwill and increase the amount of goodwill created in an M&A transaction. As previously discussed, a deferred tax liability is created in a stock sale M&A transaction due to the fact that the target's written-up assets are depreciated on a GAAP book basis but not for tax purposes. The DTL line item on the balance sheet remedies this accounting discrepancy between book basis and tax basis. It serves as a reserve account that is reduced annually by the amount of the taxes associated with the new transaction-related depreciation and amortization (i.e., the annual depreciation and amortization amounts multiplied by the company's tax rate). This annual tax payment is a real use of cash and runs through the company's statement of cash flows.

55) B. Companies often pre-screen potential acquisitions and proposed financing structures with the rating agencies to gain comfort that a given credit rating will be received or maintained. The ultimate financing structure often reflects this rating agency feedback, which may result in the company increasing the equity portion of the financing despite an adverse effect on pro forma earnings.

56) Public strategics use accretion/(dilution) analysis to measure the pro forma effects of the transaction on earnings, assuming a given purchase price and financing structure. It centers on comparing the acquirer's earnings per share (EPS) pro forma for the transaction versus on a standalone basis. The key drivers for accretion/(dilution) are purchase price, acquirer and target projected earnings, synergies, and form of financing, most notably the debt/equity mix and cost of debt. The calculations must also reflect transaction-related effects pertaining to deal structure, such as the write-up of tangible and intangible assets. As would be expected, maximum accretive effects are served by negotiating as low a purchase price as possible, sourcing the cheapest form of financing, choosing the optimal deal structure, and identifying significant achievable synergies.

57) As a general rule, acquirers do not pursue transactions that are dilutive over the foreseeable earnings projection period due to the potential destructive effects on shareholder value. There may be exceptions in certain situations, however. For example, a rapidly growing business with an accelerated earnings ramp-up in the relatively distant future years may eventually yield accretive results that do not show up in a typical two-year earnings projection time horizon.

58) Concerns over the certainty of closing and ability to finance, as well as other structural and contract issues, may cause a higher dollar value bid to be rejected in favor of a lower one.

More great resources to help you master investment banking and valuation

Welcome to the No. 1 knowledge center for M&A and capital markets professionals, professors, and students. It includes the deepest educational ancillaries and self-study tools anywhere, including a comprehensive workbook and detailed valuation models, as well as focus notes for those learning on the go.

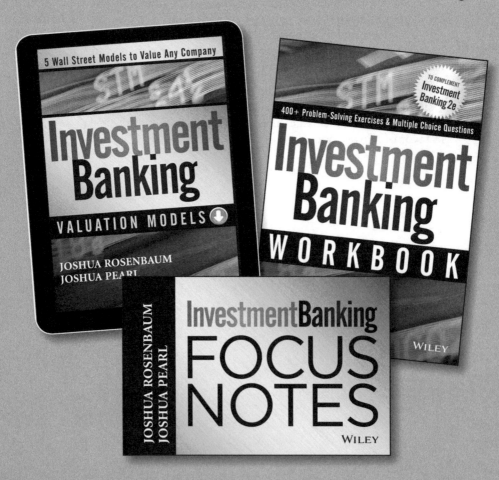

Get started at www.rosenbaumandpearl.com